THE ART OF ADAPTATION

"A thorough how-to-adapt book for the beginning and experienced writer to guide and focus feelings and thoughts to get on with the writing."
> —Malia Scotch Marmo, screenwriter, *Once Around* and *Hook*

"The perplexing problem of adapting material for a cinematic medium often hostile to the tone and style of the original has never been addressed in such specific and clear terms. Ms. Seger asks questions and identifies the problems, and those are the first steps to finding answers and solutions."
> —Frank Pierson, screenwriter, *Dog Day Afternoon* and *Presumed Innocent*

"A great book. It answers every question that pertains to fictional or factual adaptations to film. It is thorough right down to where to find a lawyer if you need assistance in securing the rights to a story. An invaluable asset to a producer."
> —Pat Finnegan, producer, Finnegan-Pinchuk Company

"The most useful book I've read on adaptation. Clear, concise, insightful."
> —Cynthia Whitcomb, coauthor, *I Know My First Name Is Steven*; author, *Selling Your Screenplay*

"Should be required reading for anyone interested in adapting other material for the screen. Clear, thorough, and extremely helpful. I highly recommend it."
> —Richard Zanuck, producer, *Driving Miss Daisy* and *Jaws*

THE ART OF
ADAPTATION

ALSO BY LINDA SEGER

Making a Good Script Great
Creating Unforgettable Characters

THE ART OF
ADAPTATION

TURNING FACT AND FICTION INTO FILM

LINDA SEGER

AN OWL BOOK

HENRY HOLT and COMPANY   NEW YORK

Henry Holt and Company, Inc.
Publishers since 1866
115 West 18th Street
New York, New York 10011

Henry Holt® is a registered trademark
of Henry Holt and Company, Inc.

Library of Congress Cataloging-in-Publication Data
Seger, Linda.
The art of adaptation : turning fact and fiction into
film / Linda Seger.—1st ed.
p.   cm.
"An Owl book."
Includes bibliographical references and index.
1. Film adaptations.   2. Motion picture authorship.
3. Motion picture plays—Technique.   4. Motion pictures
and literature.   I. Title.
PN1997.85.S44   1992
808.2'3—dc20   91-29095
                                                                CIP

ISBN 0-8050-1626-0

Henry Holt books are available for special promotions
and premiums. For details contact: Director, Special Markets.

First Edition—1992

Designed by Katy Riegel

Printed in the United States of America
All first editions are printed on acid-free paper.∞

7   9   10   8   6

Grateful acknowledgment is made to the following for permission to use the material
indicated: The William Morris Agency, Inc., on behalf of the author's estate for excerpts
from *Gone With the Wind* by Margaret Mitchell, copyright 1936, 1964 by
Margaret Mitchell; Houghton Mifflin Company for excerpts from *Deliverance* by
James Dickey, copyright © 1970 by James Dickey, all rights reserved; Martin Secker
and Warburg Limited for excerpts from *My Left Foot* by Christy Brown; New
American Library for excerpts from "The Body" in *Different Seasons* by Stephen
King, copyright © 1982.

to Peter

ACKNOWLEDGMENTS

WITH MANY THANKS

TO

my editor, Cynthia Vartan, because working with her is a joy;

TO

my agent, Martha Casselman, for her help and support;

TO

my consultant, Lenny Felder, for great advice and encouragement;

TO

Lee and Jan Batchler and Ethel Symolon, for the title, and to Gloria Stern for the title to Part Three;

TO

Karen Balog, Beth Brickell, Dara Marks, Donie Nelson, and Ed Whetmore, for reading the book and giving me such valuable comments;

TO

novelist Phyllis Gebauer, for her perceptive comments on the book, and for special help on Chapter Nine;

TO

novelist Gayle Stone and Professor David Oates, for reading and commenting on Chapter Two; Professors Wayne Rood and Joyce Cavarozzi and playwrights Dale Wasserman and Don Freed, for reading and commenting on Chapter Three; and writer Cynthia Cherbak, for brainstorming on Chapter Four;

AND TO

entertainment attorney Stephen Rohde, for sharing his knowledge and guiding me on Chapter Ten, and Philippe Perebinussoff, executive director of Broadcast Standards at ABC, for his information and help on Chapter Eleven.

A special thank-you to writer Nelson Giddings, who has written innumerable adaptations. Several years ago I attended a talk by Nelson on this subject, which helped me work out an approach to this material. Part of Chapter One is dependent upon some of Nelson's concepts, which he has allowed me to use to introduce the basic work of adaptation.

And always to my husband, Peter, to whom this book is dedicated.

CONTENTS

PREFACE

Have you ever noticed how many films are adaptations? Adaptations are the lifeblood of the film and television business. Think about how many of our great films come from books, plays, and true-life stories: *The Birth of a Nation*, *The Wizard of Oz*, *Gone With the Wind*, *The African Queen*, *Casablanca*, *Shane*, *High Noon*, and *Rear Window*, to name a few. Even the classic *Citizen Kane* was loosely based on the true-life story of William Randolph Hearst.

Most Academy Award– and Emmy Award–winning films are adaptations. Consider these amazing statistics:

- 85 percent of all Academy Award–winning Best Pictures are adaptations.
- 45 percent of all television movies-of-the-week are adaptations, yet 70 percent of all Emmy Award winners come from these films.
- 83 percent of all miniseries are adaptations, but 95 percent of Emmy Award winners are drawn from these films.

In any one year, most of the talked-about films will be adaptations. In December 1989 such films included *Sea of Love, War of the Roses, She-Devil, The Little Mermaid, Henry V, My Left Foot, The Bear, Glory, Black Rain,* and *Steel Magnolias.* Nineteen-ninety's adaptations included *Awakenings, Postcards from the Edge, Bonfire of the Vanities, Memphis Belle, Dances With Wolves, The Russia House, Henry and June, Reversal of Fortune, GoodFellas, Hamlet, Cyrano de Bergerac, The Grifters,* and *Misery.*

These adaptations are not the exclusive domain of experienced writers and big-name producers. Many new writers have gotten their start as screenwriters by optioning a book or true-life story and insisting that they be hired to write the script. Barry Morrow (*Rain Man*) optioned the true-life story of Bill (a mentally retarded man), which went on to win an Emmy Award. Anna Hamilton Phelan's first script, *Mask*, was based on the life of Rusty and Rocky Dennis (Rocky was a boy with craniodiphicil syndrome, a genetic disorder that causes severe distortions of the face). Brian Ross wrote a script on spec of a true-life story called *A Friendly Suit*, which has been optioned several times but has not yet been made. However, that script led to NBC's hiring him to write two docudramas, *Cast the First Stone* and *On Thin Ice: The Tai Babilonia Story.* Leoni Sandercook got her start with the television movie *A Season of Fear*, again a true-life story. Kurt Luedtke wrote *Out of Africa*, his second produced film, partly because he was optioning a little-known but important book about Denys Finch-Hatton, which provided the key to making *Out of Africa* workable. Earl Hamner began his career by adapting his novel into a television series, which became the long-running *The Waltons.*

Many novelists look to film to give their stories a second chance and to increase readership. Million-dollar options are no longer uncommon among the most successful novelists. New novelists, as well, hope to see their stories turned into film, often writing specifically with an eye to movie structure and characters. Pete Dexter, who wrote the best-selling novel *Paris Trout*, sold the film rights to his book on the condition that he write the screenplay.

More and more executives and producers are turning to adaptations for their film material. Many of them say that it's more commercially viable to do material that already has an audience. Others cite the paucity of good original scripts, saying that many scripts are derivative and unoriginal. But the cost can be high. Doing an adaptation means paying for the project twice—first to purchase the rights, second to pay for the screenplay. And the material needs to be evaluated twice: first the potential workability of the source material must be assessed; then it must be decided whether the screenplay is the best translation of the story.

Just as some of the greatest successes in films have been adaptations, so have some of the greatest failures. One adaptation, *Heaven's Gate*, brought down a studio (United Artists). Another, *Raise the Titanic*, was responsible for the demise of Marble Arch Productions, a once strong and successful production company. Another, *A Chorus Line*, already had over a million dollars invested in rights before the cameras rolled. Yet in spite of a record run on Broadway, audiences did not come to see the film. Obviously, a great deal rides on doing an adaptation right.

Adapting from one source to another is a process. *The Art of Adaptation* is about how to do it. This book breaks down the process to guide writers, producers, film executives, and directors who struggle with the conversion of source material to films. It can also help novelists and playwrights convert their own works into screenplays (and from my experience of consulting with novelists and playwrights, I've discovered that most of them have that desire).

This book builds on the material in my first two books, *Making a Good Script Great* and *Creating Unforgettable Characters*. You needn't have read them to be able to use this book, but if you've never written a screenplay, you will probably want to read some basic screenwriting books in addition to this one to guide you through the process (see page 226).

Most of the concepts in this book come from my own work as a consultant on a number of film adaptations, many of which are currently in development and some of which have been produced, such as *Romero*, about the archbishop of El Salvador who was assassinated in 1980; *The Neverending Story II*, based on the novel by Michael Ende; and *Flowers in the Attic*, from the V. C. Andrews book. Produced television adaptations include *Pancho Barnes* (about a woman aviator in the early days of flying), *The Fourth Wise Man* (based on the novella of the same name by Henry Van Dyke), and the Australian miniseries *The Rainbow Warrior*, about the New Zealand ship belonging to the pro-peace organization Greenpeace that was blown up by French government agents in July 1985.

Throughout the book I will be drawing on films that are well known to readers. All of these are available on video—you may want to rewatch some of them as you read the book.

If you want to return to the original source material, it can easily be found in bookstores and libraries. I have focused on fiction that I find enjoyable to read, hoping you will enjoy it too.

Most examples of novels and their film adaptations are drawn from *Gone With the Wind*, *A Room with a View*, *One Flew Over the Cuckoo's Nest*, and *Deliverance*. For examples of short-story adaptations, I refer to several that are found in the book *No, but I Saw the Movie*, edited by David Wheeler. I refer to such well-known plays and their film adaptations as *Amadeus*, *The Little Foxes*, *Driving Miss Daisy*, and *The Visit*; the latter was the focus of my dissertation project and the subject of a film in the 1950's. My examples of true-life stories made into films focus on well-known people and on films that are easily found in a video store.

Whether you are a seasoned writer or a novice, I hope this book will help you clarify the key concepts that can make the difference between an adaptation that works and one that doesn't—concepts that can make the adaptation as good as, or even better than, the original.

HOW TO USE THIS BOOK

This is a resource book. You don't need to begin at the beginning and read it straight through. If you are currently working on an adaptation, you may want to begin with the Introduction, which gives an overview of the work of the adaptor, then move directly to Part Two, which contains practical methods for translating a work's story, characters, theme, and style into film.

Part One will help you analyze your source material, so you'll understand why problems arise. If you're optioning material, you'll want to study Part Three in order to protect yourself legally.

This is a practical book. I hope it will be useful at every stage of your adaptation.

INTRODUCTION

TURNING FACT AND FICTION INTO FILM

You've read the book. It was visual, cinematic. The characters were compelling, the story involving, the style entertaining. But the film didn't work. Why?

You loved the play. It seemed like a sure thing for a film. Millions had seen it in the theatres, but audiences stayed away from the film. What went wrong?

Why is it that the worst failures and the greatest successes so often are adaptations? Why do some work and others don't? Is it that the writers and producers don't know their jobs? Or is there something intrinsic to the adaptation process that spells trouble?

In spite of what we may think, there is no such thing as an easy adaptation. We've probably all heard people say, "All you have to do is film the book." Francis Ford Coppola tried that with the 1974 version of *The Great Gatsby*, and it failed. Others say, "This was immensely popular, it's bound to be a block-buster." *Bonfire of the Vanities* was a best-seller, but the film was panned. Many writers and producers have undertaken a project that seemed to be a "sure thing," only to fail after thousands—or millions—of dollars had been spent.

By its very nature, adaptation is a transition, a conversion, from one medium to another. All original material will put up a bit of a fight, almost as if it were saying, "Take me as I am." Yet adapting implies change. It implies a process that demands rethinking, reconceptualizing, and understanding how the nature of drama is intrinsically different from the nature of all other literature.

The adaptor is much like the sculptor Michelangelo, who, when asked how he was able to carve such a beautiful angel, replied, "The angel is caught inside the stone. I simply carve out everything that isn't the angel." The adaptor is sculpting out everything that isn't drama, so the intrinsic drama contained within another medium remains.

What do you need to do to make an adaptation work? What does the process include?

CONDENSE OR EXPAND THE MATERIAL

Very few original sources will be equal to a two-hour film. The six-hundred-page novel will be too long, the short story or newspaper article will be too short. The first job of the adaptor will be to figure out how to fit the original material into different time parameters.

Rarely does a film story begin and end where the book does. True, there are notable exceptions. The film *Gone With the Wind* begins with the first scene of the book and ends with the last scene of the book. More often, though, beginnings and endings are found within the body of the story. The book *The Color Purple* begins with the first incident of incest between Celie and her father, several years before the point in time when the film begins. The film *Stand by Me* ends eleven pages before the end of the novella.

The nature of condensing involves losing material. Condensing often includes losing subplots, combining or cutting characters, leaving out several of the many themes that might be contained in a long novel, and finding within the material the beginning, middle, and end of a dramatic story line. These choices can be frustrating, since writers sometimes need to give up scenes and characters they love in order to make the film work.

Cutting and combining characters helps condense an unwieldy novel into a workable form. In the film *Gone With the Wind*, you know the characters of Scarlett O'Hara, Rhett Butler, Melanie, Ashley, Aunt Pittypat, Dr. Meade, Prissy, and Mammy. If you read the book, you would be introduced to several other important characters, such as Archie, Will, and the governor. In the book, Scarlett's mother, Ellen, was a very important figure whose values and kindnesses and images of what it meant to be a Southern lady served as both an example to Scarlett and as a reason for her considerable guilt about much of her behavior. Yet Ellen was rarely seen in the film. She needed to be sacrificed because of the length of the novel.

The work of adapting the short story demands adding rather than subtracting. Usually a short story has fewer characters than a novel, and they are in a simple situation, sometimes one without a beginning, middle, and end. In many short stories there are few, or no, subplots to complicate the action. Working with the short story demands adding subplots, adding characters, and expanding scenes and story lines.

Many of our best-known and best-loved films come from short stories. These include *Stagecoach*, *It Happened One Night*, *All About Eve*, *It's a Wonderful Life*, and *High Noon*. One of my favorite musicals, *Seven Brides for Seven Brothers*, came from the very charming short story "The Sobbin' Women" by Stephen Vincent Benét.

"The Greatest Gift," a short story by Philip Van Doren Stern that became the film *It's a Wonderful Life*, revolves around a single incident: George wants to kill himself and an angel takes him back to see how life would be without him. The screenwriter used this incident, but expanded on George's backstory and relationships. In "The Tin Star" by John M. Cunningham, which became *High Noon*, the main character dies at the end. For the film, relationships and a victorious ending were added.

For other film adaptations of short stories new scenes and situations were added to round out and develop characters and story line. In "Stage to Lordsburg" by Ernest Haycox (*Stagecoach*), the role of Ringo became a focus of the story, expanding the role for John Wayne. In the adaptation of "Night Bus" by Samuel Hopkins Adams (*It Happened One Night*), subplots were strengthened and filled out with detail.

These decisions help craft the script into a workable dramatic story line. But the adaptor also has to translate the story into a commercially viable film.

MAKING IT COMMERCIAL

For many writers, *commercial* is a dirty word. It implies compromising, losing the integrity of one's project, adding a car chase and a sex scene as a lowest common denominator to draw audiences.

It is true that for many producers and executives commercial is a very limited concept. Many studios look to the last blockbuster to define it, to *Die Hard 2*, not to *Driving Miss Daisy*, which has already grossed over $100,000,000 in business. They define it by *Total Recall*, not by *My Left Foot*, a low-budget film that has made a respectable profit. They define it by the bottom line, not by the top line—quality.

But it's important to remember that entertainment is show plus business, and producers need to be reasonably sure that they can make a profit on their investment. There is a fine line between taking reasonable risks so that original projects get made, and making cautious decisions by assessing what has drawn audiences in the past.

This fine line becomes particularly important when deciding what to adapt. There are many novels, plays, and true-life stories that are simply not commercially viable. They are too difficult to adapt and will resist any changes to make them adaptable. The adaptor and the producers need to make a reasonable assessment about what will work and what will be too difficult and not worth the investment.

Personally, I believe that many projects are adaptable. I applaud the producers and writers who stretch the art of filmmaking by finding new subject matter and new stories. I'm delighted by the surprises—the books and plays we didn't expect to work. Films like *Driving Miss Daisy*, *Amadeus*, *A Room with a View*, *Ordinary People*, and *Reversal of Fortune* all had problems implicit in the material that could have meant failure. Yet these problems were solved, proving that if you know what you're doing and do it well, unusual stories can be successful. But how do you know what to do? And how do you make a seemingly noncommercial work commercial?

A best-selling book might be read by a million readers, or perhaps four to eight million if it's one of the biggest sellers. A successful Broadway play might be seen by one to eight million people, but if only five million people go to see a film, it will be considered a failure. If only ten million people watch a television series, it will be canceled. Films and television shows need to satisfy the masses to make a profit. Novels and plays have a more select audience, so they can cater to a more elite market: they can be thematic; they can deal with esoteric issues, or work with abstract styles. But the transition to film requires that the material be accessible to the general public.

A number of decisions can make material more commercially viable. Strengthening the story line is a first step, for audiences like a well-told story. A good story has movement and focus and engages audiences from beginning to end. Most successful American films have a main character who is likable, sympathetic, and identifiable. While watching a film we like to cheer for the protagonist, wanting the best for this character and wanting him or her to achieve specific goals. We want the protagonist to win at the end. As audiences we expend considerable emotional energy wishing this character success.

A sympathetic character is not a necessity in novels and plays, but it is something filmmakers look for when they are considering material. That does not mean that a story with a negative character cannot be adapted, however, and there are several techniques that writers use to accomplish this. Sometimes understanding is substituted for sympathy. Although we don't necessarily approve of Scarlett O'Hara's manipulation or deception, we understand much of it. We understand what's driving her, why she does what she does. Although we might not admire the choices that Rusty makes in *Presumed Innocent*, we sympathize with his situation. In other cases positive characters are developed to balance the negative characters. In *Reversal of Fortune*, the sympathetic lawyer balances the decadent von Bulows. In *The Little Foxes*, the focus for the film changed from the cruel and manipulative Regina to her sympathetic daughter, Zan.

As a rule, Americans don't like their major characters to lose or to die at the end. We like happy endings. Perhaps it's part of our idealism or optimism as a country, but most American films show the villain getting his comeuppance and the hero and heroine living happily together. Part of making it commercial means knowing your market. If you are aiming for the American marketplace, you need to be careful about your endings. You need to look carefully at what kind of ending you have, and how you can make a sad ending satisfying. You might also need to gauge the spirit of the times. In 1990–91 we had a preponderance of sad endings in films, some of which were more emotionally satisfying than others. Think about how you feel about the unhappy endings of such films as *GoodFellas*, *Godfather III*, and *Awakenings*.

In making the transition to film, many books or plays that are downers have had the endings changed in order to appeal to the wider demographics of film and television.

This is not true with films from other markets. An Australian writer once explained to me why many of their main characters die at the end of their films. He said, "Your heroes always win. Lewis and Clark head out for the Oregon Territory, they explore it, and succeed in accomplishing what they set out to do. Our heroes set out to cross the desert, and they die." In 1989 I consulted on the Australian film *The Crossing*. In the script the main character survived. But as they were shooting the story they decided he needed to die—an Australian ending for an Australian film.

If you must kill off your main character (and I do not take the view that you must never do this—just be aware that it's a risky decision), make sure that there is some other emotional center in your story. Make sure that we aren't left grieving alone. Give us some other character who will grieve with us, and can help us understand the significance of the death so it becomes some higher victory. In *Love Story*, one main character died, but we saw the story through the eyes of the husband. We sympathized with him, and went through an emotional catharsis as we vicariously grieved with him over his wife's illness and death. There was a similar catharsis in *Terms of Endearment*, *Steel Magnolias*, and *Dark Victory*.

Making it more commercial also means simplifying, clarifying, sometimes spelling out a story line, and making sure that characters are not ambiguous. Novels and plays are more able to encompass ambiguities. Their story lines can meander off on tangents before coming back to the main focus. We may follow several characters and get involved in several individual lives. But film audiences can get confused if they don't know whom to root for or are unsure as to who is the main character. Although there are occasional ensemble pieces with many focal characters (such as some miniseries, or even *The Big Chill*), generally a specific character will come to the forefront. *Stand by Me* dealt with the friendship of four boys, but Gordy was the focal character. *Deliverance* was a story about the wilderness journey of four men. The movie could have been an ensemble piece, but Ed became the focal character.

Creating a commercial and viable adaptation means giving the story a clearer structure, so audiences can easily follow it. Film is usually a one-time experience. There's no opportunity to turn back the page, recheck a name, reread the description. Clarity is an important element in commercial viability.

CHANGES ARE ESSENTIAL

There is only one kind of impossible adaptation—the one where the producer and writer do not have creative license. Changes are essential in order to make the transition to another medium. Some of these changes can be minor—changing Atlanta to Charleston for budgetary reasons, for instance, or changing the name of a character whose name is the same as a current newsmaker's, or changing a train to a plane, or creating a family of three children instead of five.

Many changes are made for dramatic purposes. In the film *Rear Window*, the character of Sam, the houseman, was changed to the sassy Stella, who had an expanded role of nurse and helper. In *58 Minutes (Die Hard 2)* the daughter was changed to the wife in order to raise the stakes. In *It Happened One Night*, the situation became more serious by having a detective chase Peter and Ellie rather than just having a man on the bus recognize them.

These changes can be difficult for the original writer, who has struggled with creative choices only to see them so easily changed by the screenwriter. But not every adaptation has to follow the original. In fact, if adaptors have an exaggerated respect for every word, comma, and turn of phrase in the literature, they will be unable to re-form the material into drama.

Many successful films have used the original material simply as a jumping-off point. Very little of the book *My Left Foot* is in the film. In the book there is no restaurant scene, no art gallery exhibit, no scenes about Christy falling in love with a nurse. But the spirit of the book is there—the story of a man learning independence and developing his talents.

When screenwriters adapt nonfiction books (such as *Games Mother Never Taught You*, or *Having It All*), they will often take ideas from the book and imagine story lines that could express that theme. In *Harper Valley P.T.A.* situations from the song of the same name are used to create a drama. *Sea of Love* uses the song's image of overpowering love as a starting place for its story line.

Theatre directors are famous for using the classics to explore contemporary forms and issues. Peter Brook set his production of *A Midsummer Night's Dream* in the context of a circus. When I was a theatre director I directed *The Comedy of Errors* shortly after *Star Wars* was released. I set it in a galaxy far away, re-creating the slave twins as droids. This change demanded cutting only one page of Shakespeare's lines, which contained allusions to Belgium and France. Occasionally, contemporary adaptations of the classics have been the subjects of films. Most famous, perhaps, is the play and film *West Side Story*, which is based on *Romeo and Juliet*, or Steve Martin's updating of *Cyrano de Bergerac* in *Roxanne*.

There is no rule apart from the obligations of your contract that says you can't use your imagination when working with the original material. The adaptation is a new original. The adaptor looks for the balance between preserving the spirit of the original and creating a new form.

WHAT IS USABLE?

Adapting a story is somewhat like finding the delphiniums in a garden that includes one hundred different flowers. It means choosing what's important within material that might be very rich with complexities and a certain amount of chaos. Choices need to be made. Among all the themes, which is the one I want to explore? Among all the characters, whom do I consider the most important? Among the myriad plots and subplots, which ones are dramatically worth pursuing?

Adaptation demands choice. This means that much material that you love may be let go. Events might have to be refocused. Characters who carried a great deal of weight in the book might be deemphasized. If an important plot line doesn't serve the dramatic movement of the story, it could be dropped. With all these changes resonances may be lost, but the focus of the story line may be strengthened. A theme may be lost in order to make other themes clearer and more accessible. Making changes takes a certain amount of courage from the writer, but if writers are unwilling to make some changes in the source material, the transition from literature to drama won't happen.

The material will often fight the writer. The work of the adaptation depends, then, on understanding what is intrinsically undramatic about each form. By knowing where and why the material resists the transition, writers and producers are better able to know what material is not worth the effort, and what problems need to be addressed in order to make the adaptation work.

PART
ONE

WHAT'S THE PROBLEM?

WHY LITERATURE
RESISTS FILM

There is something delicious about reading a good book. I have been an avid reader since the age of seven. Having begun with the Bobbsey Twins and Nancy Drew, I moved to the richer fare of *Jane Eyre* and *Little Women*, *Gone With the Wind* and *To Kill a Mockingbird*.

Because of my frequent airplane trips, I have recently been reading a number of best-sellers. On my way to New Zealand I found myself stranded in Honolulu for a day because of airplane troubles, and spent the time mesmerized by *Presumed Innocent*. Curled up in a wicker chair at the Sheraton Hotel I read for hours, fascinated by the unfolding of the story, by the rich characters, and by what the book was telling me about obsession and marriage, politics and power. When I watched the film the story came to the forefront. I wanted to be able to follow every clue, to watch it unravel, and to clarify some of the parts of the book that I'd forgotten. When the film worked well, the story was clear and involving. At other times I was confused and bewildered, which lessened my enjoyment of it.

But the experience of reading a novel is quite different from watching a film. And it's exactly this difference that fights translation into film. When we read a novel, time is on our side. It is not just a chronological experience, where someone else determines our pacing, but a reflective experience. Rarely do we read a novel in one sitting. In fact, part of the joy of reading is going back to the book. The reading, putting it down, thinking about it, sometimes reading a page twice is part of the pleasure. It is a reveling in the language as much as reveling in the story.

THE IMPORTANCE OF THEME

Novels, unlike films or plays, communicate all their information through words. The words express much more than story and events, images and character—they express ideas. Occasionally you do see a novel that is purely story—usually a short novel that's not particularly known for its literary merits. All of the great novels, however, and most of the good ones, are not just telling a story but are pursuing an idea. They are about something significant, and this theme is just as important as the story line, if not more so.

The best films also have strong themes, but in a film the theme serves the story. It's there to reinforce and dimensionalize the story, not to replace it. In a novel, the story often serves the theme.

The book *Gone With the Wind* is as much about the lost South as it is about Scarlett's relationships and struggles. The theme gives depth to the story. When I watch the film, however, the story sweeps me along. The story becomes the most important and the idea about the lost South is not what I remember best. I remember Scarlett and Rhett and the burning of Atlanta and Melanie and Ashley.

The novel gives me many more layers. It follows its thematic line by building up detail after detail, page after page, about the manners and rituals and parties and hierarchies of the South. Even the characters reinforce the theme. In passages such as the following, the characters are defined thematically, in terms of how they relate to the Old South.

> Although born to the ease of plantation life, waited on hand and foot since infancy, the faces of the three on the porch [Scarlett and the Tarleton twins] were neither slack nor soft. They had the vigor and alertness of country people who have spent all their lives in the open and troubled their heads very little with dull things in books. Life in the north Georgia county of Clayton was still new and, according to the standards of Augusta, Savannah and Charleston, a little crude. The more sedate and older sections of the South looked down their noses at the upcountry Georgians, but here in north Georgia, a lack of the niceties of classical education carried no shame, provided a man was smart in the things that mattered. And raising good cotton, riding well, shooting straight, dancing lightly, squiring the ladies with elegance and carrying one's liquor like a gentleman were the things that mattered.

As the book unfolds, we see the disappearance of this way of life and how the characters react to the New South. Scarlett, through many compromises, is able to bend with the new era of Reconstruction. The book-loving, less practical Ashley is not. Rhett finds his integrity in the New South. Frank Kennedy becomes a hero while trying to preserve certain values of the Old South. In the beginning of the film *Gone With the Wind*, words on a scroll sum up this important theme from the book:

> *There was a land of Cavaliers and Cotton Fields*
> *called the Old South . . .*
> *Here in this patrician world the*
> *Age of Chivalry took its last bow . . .*
>
> *Here was the last ever to be seen*
> *of Knights and their Ladies Fair,*
> *of Master and Slave . . .*

Look for it only in books, for it
is not more than a dream remembered,
a Civilization gone with the wind . . .

As the novel explores the idea of the lost South, it also takes its time giving us other layers of the story.

BUILDING UP DETAIL

Have you ever noticed that a book may take fifty or one hundred pages to give you the information that you get in three minutes of film? In *Bonfire of the Vanities*, the events in the first fourteen minutes of the film take up about eighty-nine pages in the book. When I worked on the adaptation of *Christy* by Catherine Marshall, the first image we created for the film corresponded to thirty-two pages of the book. Even in a short novel such as *58 Minutes* (the basis of the film *Die Hard 2*), it took forty-six pages in the book to create what we see in the first few minutes of the film. In *Gone With the Wind*, what happens in the first one hundred twenty-seven pages of the book is presented to us in less than thirty minutes of film.

Film is much faster. It builds up its details through images. The camera can look at a three-dimensional object and, in a matter of seconds, get across details that would take pages in the novel. Film can give us story information, character information, ideas and images and style all in the same moment.

When we read a novel, we can see only what the narrator shows us at that particular moment. If the narrator puts the focus on action in those pages, then we follow the action. If the narrator talks about feelings, then we focus on the feelings. We can receive only one piece of information at a time. A novel can only give us this information sequentially.

But film is dimensional. A good scene in a film advances the action, reveals character, explores the theme, and builds an image. In a novel, one scene or an entire chapter may concentrate on only one of those areas.

In the process of building up details, the novel is also communicating other information. When the novel *Gone With the Wind* takes several paragraphs to describe Ashley Wilkes, it is giving us important character information. But it's also using words to convey ideas about the kind of life Ashley was meant for—a gentleman's life in the Old South. It is building up details that will pay off in the last half of the book. Read this descriptive passage in which Gerald O'Hara describes Ashley:

> Our people and the Wilkes are different. . . . They are queer folk, and it's best that they marry their cousins and keep their queerness to themselves. . . . And when I say queer, it's not crazy I'm meaning. He's not queer like the Calverts who'd gamble everything they have on a horse, or the Tarletons who turn out a drunkard or two in every litter, or the Fontaines who are hot-headed little brutes and after murdering a man for a fancied slight. . . . But he's queer in other ways. . . . Now, Puss, tell me true, do you understand his folderol about books and poetry and music and oil paintings and such foolishness?

Later, Ashley laments his lack of skills as he says to Scarlett:

> I don't want allowances made for me. I want to stand on my own feet for what I'm worth. What have I done with my life, up till now? . . . I've been thinking. I don't believe I really thought from the time of the surrender until you went away from here. I was in a state of suspended animation and it was enough that I had something to eat and a bed to lie on. But when you went to Atlanta, shouldering a man's burden, I saw myself as much less than a man—much less, indeed, than a woman. Such thoughts aren't pleasant to live with and I do not intend to live with them any longer. . . . This is my last chance. . . . If I go to Atlanta and work for you, I'm lost forever.

This character information connects ideas in various parts of the book. It builds up details and ideas about the Old South and the New South, about the world that has gone with the wind, about a man who can't adjust to the new world, and a woman who can.

THE WORK OF THE NARRATOR

As we read a novel, someone is taking us by the hand and leading us through the story. This narrator is sometimes a character (if the novel is in the first person) or the storyteller (usually the writer's alter ego), who explains to us the meaning of the events.

When the narrator in *Gone With the Wind* tells us about the "pleasant land of white houses, peaceful plowed fields and sluggish yellow rivers . . . a land of contrasts, of brightest sun glare and densest shade," the white columned house isn't there just as descriptive image; rather, the narrator is slowly giving us the details to help us understand what the world was like, and what the world would be losing. The cinematographer might show the exact same detail, but there is not the explanation with it to help us understand its deeper symbolic meaning. The narrator, however, is explaining and clarifying the connections.

In many eighteenth-century novels, the narrator made him- or herself known to the reader. It was not unusual for the narrator to interrupt the story to lecture the "dear reader" and to tell readers what they are supposed to learn from the book. Henry Fielding, the author of *Tom Jones*, published in 1749, spends some time giving us insights into human nature. He then compliments himself on his astute observations by writing:

> As this is one of those deep observations which very few
> readers can be supposed capable of making themselves,
> I have thought proper to lend them my assistance; but
> this is a favour rarely to be expected in the course of my
> work. Indeed, I shall seldom or never so indulge him,
> unless in such instances as this, where nothing but the

inspiration with which we writers are gifted can possibly enable any one to make the discovery.

The narrator of *A Room with a View*, by E. M. Forster, has a less obtrusive function, as he continually keeps us informed that this is a novel about the theme of identity. He makes comments such as "It so happened that Lucy, who found daily life rather chaotic, entered a more solid world when she opened the piano"; and later, "She was accustomed to have her thoughts confirmed by others or, at all events, contradicted; it was too dreadful not to know whether she was thinking right or wrong." The narrator of *Gone With the Wind* reminds us of character details by telling us that "Scarlett O'Hara was not beautiful, but men seldom realized it when caught by her charm." In these cases, the narrator is calling attention to what we're supposed to notice, clarifying the issues, explaining the ideas, and telling us what is happening in the story.

A narrator can move in and out of a character's life, even going inside a character's head to let us know how the character thinks and feels. This technique helps us understand even a negative character, eliciting our compassion because we have an inside view of motivation and emotions. We identify with the character psychologically, emotionally, and in terms of the action she or he takes.

In a novel, the narrator stands between us and the story to help us understand and interpret events. When we watch a film, we are an objective observer of the actions. What we see is what we get. Even if characters tell us their feelings through a voice-over in a film, we may not believe them. Without the narrator to guide us, we may not know whether characters are lying or not.

Does it matter? Yes, because we can trust the narrator in a novel, but we don't always trust the character. The narrator is omniscient. If the narrator of *A Room with a View* tells us that Lucy is really in love with George, we believe him. After all, he knows her better than we do, probably even better than Lucy knows herself. But in the film, if Lucy tells us that she doesn't love George, we don't know for sure whether to believe her. Perhaps she doesn't understand her own motives. Perhaps she's lying. Perhaps she only thinks that she doesn't love George in order to justify her engagement to Cecil. Lucy is not a trustworthy source. The narrator is.

Any attempt to translate this interior understanding into film usually meets with failure. Film doesn't give us an interior look at a character. A novel does.

THE REFLECTIVE VOICE

What else do we discover by going within a character's head? A character, as well as the narrator, is able to give us insights into the human condition. The narrator can help us understand the character's psychology and help us understand all types of characters—from the inside out.

In the novel *Ordinary People*, by Judith Guest, the character of Conrad (the young man who tries to commit suicide after the drowning of his brother) discusses the tension and unspoken problems in the family:

> This house. Too big for three people. Straining, he can barely hear the early-morning sounds of his father and mother organizing things, synchronizing schedules at the other end of the hall. It doesn't matter. He doesn't need to hear, and they would certainly not be talking about anything important. They would not be talking, for instance, about him. They are people of good taste. They do not discuss a problem in the presence of the problem. And besides, there is no problem. There is just Phase Two. Recovery. A moving forward.

Note how the author carefully uses words as "synchronizing schedules" and "anything important" and "the problem" to build up the idea that the family avoids facing problems. There is no way to get across this type of detail in a film.

THE NOVEL AS INFORMATION

Details in a novel build ideas, but they also give us information that is useful and often fascinating in itself. This may be pages of information about whales (as in *Moby-Dick*) or information about outbreaks of contagious diseases (as in Robin Cook's novel *Outbreak*) or information about plantation life.

In *Gone With the Wind*, one of the most exciting scenes is the burning of Atlanta. It occurs shortly after the memorable image of Scarlett walking among the wounded as she searches for Dr. Meade. In the book, the narrator describes this scene:

> Lying in the pitiless sun, shoulder to shoulder, head to feet, were hundreds of wounded men, lining the tracks, the sidewalks, stretched out in endless rows under the car shed. Some lay stiff and still but many writhed under the hot sun, moaning. Everywhere, swarms of flies hovered over the men, crawling and buzzing in their faces, everywhere was blood, dirty bandages, groans, screamed curses of pain as stretcher bearers lifted men. The smell of sweat, of blood, of unwashed bodies, of excrement rose up in waves of blistering heat until the fetid stench almost nauseated her. The ambulance men hurrying here and there among the prostrate forms frequently stepped on wounded men, so thickly packed were the rows, and those trodden upon stared stolidly up, waiting their turn.

That is a brilliant image. Most of the image is easily translated into film (although not, perhaps fortunately, the sense of smell). In the film, it also gains meaning as the camera draws back, stopping as the Confederate flag frames the shot. The scope, complexity, texture, sights, and sounds of the scene are particularly well translated into a strong cinematic image.

In the book, however, we get much more information about the meaning of this scene. Why were there suddenly so many wounded? What was happening during the Civil War at this time? Why did Melanie and Scarlett need to leave? What was

Sherman's plan? What was the Confederates' plan? Why was the Atlanta victory essential to the North if it was to win this war? What was in the city that was so important to both North and South?

In the book, we also learn information about the generals' strategy: the seventy-six-day battle of General Johnston, as he tried to defend Atlanta; his replacement by General Hood, and the Yankee advance on Atlanta as they tried to cut off the railroad; the thirty-day shelling of the city, and the silence that followed. And we learn that September 1, the day Melanie had her baby, was also the day that Atlanta fell.

When I watch the film, I get a sense of the sweep of the story, the excitement, terror, fear, panic, hysteria, desperation. When I read the book, I get this same sense, but I also gain new understanding of the historical period—the context, the meaning of the battles, and the strategy of both Sherman and the Confederate generals Johnston and Hood. Since the book has taken longer to build up details, it also has taken longer to make its impact. And the impact is emotional, historical, and informational.

TIME MOVEMENT IS FLUID

As the narrator leads me through the book, she or he is also able to help me understand the connection between details, ideas, and information that may appear in different chapters. The narrator can help me connect the past, present, and future.

Most novels and short stories are written in the past tense. Authors write "she said," "he went," "she thought," and only rarely write "she says," "he goes," "she thinks." In most cases, the narrator is looking back on events that have already happened and is both telling and interpreting the events to the reader.

Occasionally an author emphasizes the relationship of the event in the past to future events. In Stephen King's *Dead Zone*, the narrator sounds as if he is speaking about events that have just taken place. Then he surprises us, sounding almost as if he were looking into the future by telling us, "It was four and a half years before she talked to Johnny Smith again." In this case, it becomes clear that the narrator is not talking about a story that unfolded in the immediate past, but a story that happened at least four and a half years ago.

In a novel time is fluid. It moves back and forth among past, present, and future. A character in the present can give us information about the past. In *Gone With the Wind* the narrator tells us about Ellen's backstory, and her love for a man who left her long ago. On the rebound she married Gerald O'Hara. Years later, when Ellen died, it was not Gerald's name that was on her lips, but the name of Phillippe, her love of long ago. In itself, this particular detail is not highly important, nor is it necessary to know in the film. But backstory enriches a novel. Rather than proceeding chronologically, through words the novel moves deeper and deeper into an event, showing how any one event has meanings that encompass both the past and the present.

Fiction surrounds the event with a certain amount of reflection and context. It uses a fluid sense of time to put the action into perspective. Fiction can move back and forth from backstory to frontstory. One event can remind a character of another in the past. The narrator can describe an event by bridging the past and the present. In *Bleak House* Charles Dickens gives a description of Esther Summerson, who is recovering from a near-death illness. Notice the smooth transitions between past and present in this quote (I've marked them to show this movement back and forth):

> My hair had not been cut off, though it had been in danger more than once [past]. . . . I put my hair aside and looked at the reflection in the mirror, encouraged by seeing how placidly it looked to me [present]. I was very much changed—oh, very, very much. . . . I had never been a beauty and had never thought myself one, but I had been very different from this. It was all gone now [past]. Heaven was so good to me that I could let it go with a

few not bitter tears and could stand there arranging my hair for the night quite thankfully" [present].

In novels, this movement between the past and the present is fluid and not disruptive. The flashback is part of the movement of a story.

In film, this kind of flashback to a backstory can stop the flow of a story. Film takes place in the present. It's immediate. It's now. It's active. A novel may be reflective—emphasizing meaning, context, or response to an event—but a film puts the emphasis on the event itself.

Film works in the present and drives to the future. It's less interested in what's happened than in what's going to happen next. In some films this movement to the future is a slow unfolding. In others we almost feel ourselves catapulted forward toward the inevitable and important climax. When we watch a film, we are in the same position as the characters. We, like they, don't know what will happen next. There's no time to think about what's happening. There's only time to experience, to be involved in the unfolding of events.

Since film is immediate, we observe the story without needing a narrator's help to interpret or tell us what we're seeing.

POINT OF VIEW

The novel also focuses our attention by telling the story from a certain point of view: Whose story is it? Through whose viewpoint do we see the story unfolding?

Ken Kesey's *One Flew Over the Cuckoo's Nest* is really the story of McMurphy, who thought he could make his prison sentence easier by finishing it out in a mental institution. It's about what he does, what happens to him, how he affects others. But the novel tells the story through the viewpoint of Chief Bromden, the seemingly deaf and dumb Indian who observes the events, reflects on them, gets scared about them, worries over McMurphy, and tells us what he's noticing. Although the focus remains on McMurphy, the point-of-view character is Chief Bromden. We read about his internal thoughts and feelings as well as the external reality that he observes. This splits the emphasis in the novel. Although we focus on McMurphy's actions, we are always mindful about how we are seeing the story. We never see anything in the novel that Bromden does not personally see. We see scenes without McMurphy, but we don't see scenes without Bromden.

Ordinary People is essentially Conrad's story, as he struggles to put his life together after his brother's death and his own near suicide. This novel is not told in the first person, but by a partially omniscient narrator, who chooses to tell us about what goes on inside the head of both Conrad and his father, Calvin, but doesn't go inside the head of Beth, or other characters. Since the point of view is broader, we can see scenes without Calvin, scenes without Conrad, and scenes without either of them.

In both these examples, the story has subjective, internal elements that bring us into the thoughts and feelings of characters, rather than just telling us about external realities.

Many writers like to bring the narrator from the book into the film to give the film a more "literary" feel or to help convey information or transitions in time. *Out of Africa, Bonfire of the Vanities, GoodFellas, To Kill a Mockingbird*, and *Julia* (among many others) all used narrators. Although there are times when this technique is used to add a reflective dimension to the film, it's more usually applied to give information that could be conveyed in more dramatic ways. In many cases, the technique works against the immediacy of film, separating the audience from the action by putting the emphasis on what is said, not on what is happening.

The narrator in the novel tells us about a subjective experience, but the film, through its visuals, shows us an objective experience. In a film the voice-over narrator may tell us how someone is feeling. But this voice-over may be disruptive because we're trying to concentrate on the objective expression on a character's face. If the narrator's words contradict what we see, it may confuse us. If they tell us what we're already seeing, then we don't need the words.

I found this particularly bothersome in *Bonfire of the Vanities*, where I questioned the use of the narrator, who often dissipated the emotional focus of the film by putting the emphasis on words, not action. I was more intrigued with watching the action than with listening to someone interpret it for me.

Sometimes film uses a narrator to provide transitions. Although this is a helpful technique, there are more dramatic and imagistic methods available. In *Driving Miss Daisy* we got through twenty-five years of transitions without the use of a narrator, proving it can be done.

A film, like a novel, also presents a point of view, but to determine whose point of view the screenwriter asks different questions than the novelist. The screenwriter asks, "To what extent do I focus only on one character's world, thereby only showing scenes that contain that particular character? To what extent do I work as a more omniscient teller of the story by spreading the focus among several characters?" In the film *Ordinary People* either Conrad or Calvin was in every scene. In *One Flew Over the Cuckoo's Nest* McMurphy or Chief Bromden was in every scene.

A filmmaker might decide to broaden the point of view by showing us some scenes of a villain planning a crime, of the protagonist trying to solve the crime, and perhaps of the love interest reflecting on why her sweetheart spends so much time solving crimes instead of paying attention to her.

Sometimes the point of view is the same in both novel and film, as with *The Color Purple*, *Shane*, and *Rear Window*, and sometimes the point of view changes. The novel *Deliverance* is told from Ed's point of view, but as there are scenes without Ed in the film, it splits its point of view between Ed and Lewis. Although the novel *A Room with a View* focuses on Lucy, the film spreads the point of view. Most scenes include Lucy (as would be expected, since she's the main character), but there are some scenes without her, such as the one between Miss Lavish and Miss Bartlett, a scene of George walking home in the rain, a scene of Cecil putting on his shoes, and even a flashback scene when Cecil describes meeting the Emersons and telling them about the house for rent. This last scene, however, seemed to me to spread the point of view too much, since it meant going inside Cecil's head to show us Cecil remembering the experience. We do go inside Lucy's head several times, as she flashes back to the kiss, and that's appropriate because she's our main character. It's less appropriate to go inside Cecil's head for a flashback about his experience. You may want to watch the film again to see what you think about this change in point of view.

SUMMARY

Novels and films express themselves in different ways. Fiction uses words to tell a story, describe character, and build ideas. Films use image and action. They are essentially different mediums that resist each other as often as they cooperate.

CASE STUDY:
Field of Dreams

Field of Dreams, written and directed by Phil Alden Robinson, was adapted from the book *Shoeless Joe* by W. P. Kinsella. In 1990 the film was nominated by the Academy of Motion Picture Arts and Sciences for Best Adapted Screenplay, Best Director, and Best Picture. It is a book that many considered unadaptable. I talked to Phil about his approach to the book.

"One day," he said, "Lindsay Doran, who was an executive at Avco-Embassy, said to me, 'I have this great book you've got to read.' I asked, 'What's it about?' She said, 'It's about this guy who hears a voice.' And I said, 'Stop, not interested.' She then went on to tell me that the voice tells Ray to build a baseball field and that he kidnaps J. D. Salinger, and the more she said, the more I hated it. She begged me to read the book. Finally I agreed. I took it home, and it's the only time in my life that I couldn't put a book down. I loved it. I loved how audacious it is to start a book where a man hears a voice in the first paragraph that tells him to build a baseball field, and decides to follow it. When he goes to his wife, I expected her to tell him he's crazy, but she says, 'Well, if you feel you have to, then do it.' I thought that's the most original wife I've ever read. I thought, 'This is a movie.'

"The book was very visual. The vision of a baseball field carved out of a cornfield was beautiful. Shoeless Joe showing up at night was wonderful. I saw in it many things that I love in movies: great characters and heart and emotions and surprises.

"When I started working on the screenplay, I decided that the ending should be a surprise to Ray and to the audience. In the first chapter of the book, the father is discussed, and he arrives about two-thirds of the way through the book. If I put off his arrival until the end, then the story becomes a mystery. 'Why is Ray hearing these voices and why is he doing these tasks?' At the end, he learns that all of this was to lead to reconciling with his father.

"Most films start with a character knowing what his problem is, and then having to take steps to solve it. This is a character who doesn't find out until the end of the movie what it's all about.

"I gave Ray more questioning and skepticism in the movie so that the mystery is never too far from the audience's mind. When I wrote the first draft, I bought two copies of the paperback book and cut all the pages out and pasted them into a looseleaf book and wrote a screenplay that was from the book. I used the author's scene descriptions and dialogue as much as possible. I started on page one with Ray hearing the voice and deciding to build the field. I showed it to Lindsay Doran, who said, 'This guy's crazy.' Even though I had followed the book, the book had more backstory, more information about Ray so we get to understand him better. So I wrote a prologue to give more history of Ray and his family. And then, just in case the audience missed it, I gave him the line 'I've never done a crazy thing in my whole life.'

"I felt I needed to give Ray more resistance to the voice, because the audience would resist it, and if he doesn't, they'll wonder about him. I kept asking myself, 'What would I do if I heard a voice?' I would first assume there's a logical explanation. He asks his wife if there was a sound from a truck on the highway, or kids with a radio. At first he shrugs it off, but then it starts to bother him. In the movie, we added a scene where he goes to an ear doctor to have his hearing checked, but it turned out to be unnecessary. When we screened the movie for audiences, they were already with it. They didn't need that extra beat.

"I also gave Annie [the wife] a little more skepticism than she had in the book. She makes jokes about it.

"But when he hears the voice that sends him to Boston, I needed her to go along with this, so I created a dream for her where she dreamt she saw Ray at Fenway Park with Terence Mann. When she hears that Ray had the same dream, that was enough to overcome her skepticism. Several times in the script I have him repeat that he doesn't know why this is happening. I felt I needed that dialogue once in a while to acknowledge to the audience that the character knows this is crazy.

"I cut the film very tight so there wasn't much time for the audience to sit back and think. I didn't want to have long sequences where the audience would have time to ask questions, or decide that something didn't make sense. I wanted them to stay caught up in what Ray is caught up in. And the way to do that is to keep the film moving.

"I combined the characters of Mark, Bluestein, and Ray's twin brother into Mark, Annie's brother. He's the villain of the piece, but I had him played as the nicest person on earth who really believes he's saving his sister and brother-in-law by buying the farm. I cut out a character called Eddie 'Kid' Scissons who's an old-timer from Ray's town, presumably someone who had played in the major leagues—although later we discover that was just a story he told. He's a wonderful character, but I have this theory about what I call 'cul-de-sacs' in stories. It's like you're going straight down a road, and you leave the main road and take one of these cul-de-sacs, but when you return, you're back just where you left off. I realized this Scissons character was not going to help move us closer to the end of the story. This was something I could lift out without hurting the film.

"In the book, Ray kidnaps J. D. Salinger. I wanted to change this. I knew we'd have legal problems and I felt that using a real person's name would take us out of the movie because almost everything else was fictionalized. Well, Shoeless Joe and Archie Graham were real, but they're not people we know much about in real life.

"In the first few drafts, I just wrote the character as Salinger because I was juggling so many other things. Then I wrote another character who was a pale imitation of Salinger, and I realized that I didn't have a clue who this guy was and what he was doing. So, for the first time in my life, I thought, 'What actor would it be fun to see in this role?' My first thought was he should be a big guy. A really big guy. I had just seen James Earl Jones on Broadway in *Fences*, and I thought I'd like to see someone have to try to kidnap James Earl Jones, and then the whole scene came to me full blown.

"I wondered, 'Who is this guy?' I can make him more than just a novelist. I decided to make him a famous sixties icon—a civil rights, antiwar activist. Then after I created this character, I realized that without James Earl Jones, it was a totally lily-white movie. In a movie that purports to be about America and about baseball, his presence became even more important.

"Since I was creating a new character [Terence Mann], I had to set him up for the audience. In the book, when Ray says, 'I know whose pain I have to ease: J. D. Salinger!' it hits like a lightning bolt. But now I had to create all this information about this fictionalized character. So I added the scene at the school where they're considering banning his books. During that scene, Ray realizes whose pain he has to ease—Terence Mann. And the audience needs to know who that is. Then Annie says to Ray, 'What does this have to do with baseball?' so Ray goes to the library and does some research about Mann, which gave me a chance to add more information about this character.

"I felt this book was really steeped in the sixties spirit—about a guy who's facing a problem that all of us who are forty-something have—'What do we do with all those ideals and dreams and feelings that really defined our generation and that we're proud of having? Can you still hang on to your dreams when you get older?' Creating Terence Mann as a sixties icon helped get across part of what the movie was about.

"In the book, the players leave the field by going through a door in the outfield fence. We had all these special effects companies saying to us, 'We'll use video beams and laser zaps as they disappear,' and the production designer was drawing diagrams of the outfield fence, but none of them looked right. Then I realized what was wrong. Why would a farmer who's struggling for money spend time and money to build a fence in the outfield? Let's just let the corn serve as 'the fence.' And I decided that instead of lasers and such, we needed to be simple—they just disappear, they just fade out.

"One trick to doing this kind of film is to treat it as if it's real. It's important to keep it simple. Somebody defined the movie as magical realism. I expect they saw it as a film about magic and fantasy, but I never wanted to play into that. It's told totally realistically. It's actually somewhat similar in spirit to *Close Encounters of the Third Kind* by Stephen Spielberg, which is about a character who has a vision and resists it and then finally goes along with it.

"While writing the screenplay, whenever I was in doubt, I would trust the book. That's what got me there. One of my goals was for people to feel about the movie the way I felt about the book.

"Thankfully, Bill Kinsella [the author] was very happy with the film. While I was writing the screenplay, I had a nightmare about people who loved the book coming after me with knives.

I was nervous about what Bill would think so I sent him a long letter, explaining that I felt I needed to make certain changes—such as moving the father to the end, changing J. D. Salinger, etc., and I hoped he wouldn't mind too terribly much. He sent back a postcard, 'Dear Phil, do whatever you have to, to make it a movie. Love, Bill.' "

WHY THEATRE RESISTS FILM

Theatre is magical. Beginning with the first play I ever saw, I was entranced. I have vague memories of tall men dressed as soldiers, of the chorus singing the song "Sweethearts" (from the play *Blossom Time*) and, as we filed out, of passing the actors on their way to their dressing rooms. They seemed like wondrous people, and I stared, as seven-year-olds are asked not to do.

Many theatre performances have moved me. *A Chorus Line* inspired me to remain in drama, at a time when that decision meant great sacrifices. *One Flew Over the Cuckoo's Nest* silenced me by its power and impact. *The Caucasian Chalk Circle* overwhelmed me by its richness of theme and color, and Stacey Keach's performance in *Cyrano de Bergerac* made an incredible situation believable.

When theatre works, we come away from it moved, touched, swept up, involved. Our feelings and our intellect are engaged. We are captivated.

As a former theatre director, I know that some nights theatre happens, some nights it doesn't. When it doesn't work, the theatre is a dead, tedious, and uninspiring space. It is movement by rote, performed by sleepy actors walking through their lines and movements. Whether theatre is bad or good doesn't depend on whether it's acted by professionals or amateurs. One of the most exciting performances I've seen was a high school production of *Oklahoma!* One of my most tedious theatre evenings was spent watching a New York touring company perform *A Little Night Music.*

Theatre is more than a play. Like the screenplay, the play is a blueprint, a catalyst for another art form to emerge. It is a particular integration of talents and a relationship between audience and actors that creates theatre. Adapting the play is not the same as adapting a novel or short story, which are art forms in themselves. The play is not the art form until it's gone through its magical transformation into theatre.

But where does this magic come from? What makes theatre work?

THEATRE: AN EXCHANGE BETWEEN ACTOR AND AUDIENCE

Although the beginnings of theatre are a mystery, "acting out" seems to be a natural human expression that can be traced back thousands of years. The early Egyptians and Persians acted out rituals that celebrated the life and death and rebirth of the land. These rituals' dramatic structure showed this sequence and coincided with the flooding of the Nile.

The Greeks enacted rituals in praise of Dionysus, the god of fertility and wine. The epic poems of Homer, which were stories about the gods and men, were originally sung by only one person. Later, another actor joined the storytelling, adding dialogue and telling the stories through action, rather than speech.

Several hundred years after Homer, the Greeks began their day-long theatre celebrations. The entire town would come to watch reenactments of the great tragic stories as well as broad comic improvisations and plays about satyrs, who were half man, half animal.

In some of the early Persian and Egyptian enactments the entire community participated. In other rituals there was a differentiation between actor and audience, but the audience was not simply a group of people watching—the audience participated emotionally. There was an exchange of energy between actor and audience. Aristotle spoke about tragedy as a purgation of the basic emotions of fear and pity. Watching theatre was cathartic, for the individual and for the community. Although the form of theatre changed, the spirit remained. It's this spirit that is captured by the script of the play, and carried through between actor and audience in the performance.

When audiences enter a theatre, they give themselves over to involvement in this special world. They take part in an exchange of energy that happens among the actors, and between the actors and the audience. Some theatregoers describe the experience of watching great drama as invigorating, others as leaving them feeling physically exhausted. Some talk about a hypnotic absorption in the proceedings on stage, or a rapt attention that makes them feel in tune with the actors and the unfolding drama. I have sometimes almost stopped breathing while watching a play, as if the actor were weaving such a magical spell that I dared not breathe or I would destroy the fragile moment.

This particular dynamic between actors and audiences can't be captured by any other medium. When I directed the play *The Visit* as part of my doctoral dissertation project, several people asked me if I had filmed the play, to create a permanent record of my theatre project. I told them that you can't make a record of theatre, because once you're recorded it, it's no longer theatre, but film. It is the nature of theatre to disappear with nothing but the memory of the experience. There is no way of recording, or even explaining, what happens on the nights when the play, the actors, and the audience all work together to create this energy. Theatre is an art form carved in snow. It is impossible to preserve anything more than the experience itself.

THEATRE IS THEMATIC

Theatre turns a microscope upon the human condition. Hamlet used another metaphor, speaking of "turning a mirror up to [human] nature" by focusing on those themes that are human-centered. This is what theatre does best. Theatre tends to be more thematic than film. It does not need a strong story line to work. Many playwrights begin with a philosophy, inventing their characters to embody the theme they want to explore. Others create characters with a problem, looking at the human condition by exploring their struggles, dreams, fears, and desires.

Theatre does less well with the large tapestries of a *War and Peace* or a *Gone With the Wind*; the latter, for instance, about the passing of an old order, would not do well as a play. Yet Chekhov's *The Cherry Orchard*, about the selling of the old family home and cherry orchard, is also about the passing of an old order, but it works well as a theatre subject. Why? Because one is concerned about the larger tapestry of a social, political order; the other makes its subject small, personal, and intimate. *Gone With the Wind* looks beyond Scarlett's concerns to Southern rituals and life-styles and the land and the politics. To do that, it needs both a rich cast of characters and a wide-angle lens that can scan all the images that convey that theme.

The Cherry Orchard turns a microscope upon the similar passing of an old order. It looks at the theme worked out on a human scale. It looks at how the human being grapples with change—copes, justifies, rails, and reacts against.

Even the broader tapestries of many of Shakespeare's history plays or a historical play such as *The Royal Hunt of the Sun* still keep the human subject in focus. The sweep of events isn't as important as the human psychology and interactions of King Richard the Third, Prince Hal, or Pizarro.

When theatre tries to do too much and moves away from the human focus, it dissipates its energy. Audiences become lost and disinterested. The magic disappears.

36

THEATRE EXPLORES
HUMAN-CENTERED THEMES

Theatre does much better than film at exploring both internal human struggles and broad human themes. If you wanted to explore the dreams, concerns, strivings, and yearnings that are common to all artists, you might write a play like *A Chorus Line* (written with the help of dancers and a long-running tape recorder). If you wanted to explore the interaction between the human and the divine, you might write *Jesus Christ Superstar*. And if you wanted to explore a psychiatrist yearning for a lost passion for life, you might write *Equus*.

Notice, none of these great plays made particularly good films. At their most basic, they were highly theatrical pieces. The theatrical space, the spectacle, and the energy between audience and actors—everything that made them great theatre was untranslatable into film.

THEATRE CAN USE
ABSTRACT SETS AND SPACES

Theatre doesn't need realism to work. Molière said that all he needed was a "platform and a passion or two." Thornton Wilder said that all he needed for the climax of his play *Our Town* was "only five square feet of boarding and the passion to know what life means to us." All that is necessary in theatre is a space for dramatic interaction.

In fact, as long as the human being remains paramount in a theatrical work, the actual sets can be quite nonrepresentational, even abstract. When we enter the theatre we know that we have entered an artificial, symbolic space. The three walls clearly are not a house, the two flags represent the whole army, and the three boxes only suggest a carriage. When we enter the theatre, we have already suspended our disbelief. We are already making a leap of imagination.

THEATRE USES FLUID SPACE

In theatre, the space is fluid. Peter Brook says in *The Empty Space*:

> The absence of scenery in the Elizabethan theatre was one of its greatest freedoms. . . . Their cinematic structure of alternating short scenes, plot intercut with subplot, were all part of a total shape. This shape is only revealed dynamically, that is, in the uninterrupted sequence of these scenes. Compared to the cinema's mobility, the theatre once seemed ponderous and creaky, but the closer we move towards the true nakedness of theatre, the closer we approach a stage that had a lightness and range far beyond film or television."

In theatre, actors move easily from space to space. On one corner of the stage, we accept that they're in a field, at the other, that they're in a castle. Theatre has no need for the realism of film. In fact, realism can interrupt the action and destroy the magic.

Plays that are particularly well known for their theatricality depend on this fluid abstract space. Sometimes this space covers great distances, such as in *Henry V*, where armies are on the battlefields of England and France, or *The Royal Hunt of the Sun*, about the conquest of Peru by Pizarro. In *Driving Miss Daisy*, the space is used to represent a car, a home, a graveyard, a supermarket.

Sometimes this space is generalized—we don't know quite where we are. In *Godspell* we are . . . where? On a road? In a room? By a fence? It doesn't matter. The play *Children of a Lesser God* takes place "in the mind of James Leeds. Throughout the events characters step from his memory for anything from a full scene to several lines. The stage is bare, holding only a few benches and a blackboard and permitting characters to appear and disappear easily."

Theatre is fluid even when it takes place in an enclosed space.

These small spaces provide a tight focus for the characters, intensifying what they are doing and revealing.

Steel Magnolias takes place in a beauty parlor, *One Flew Over the Cuckoo's Nest* in a "Day Room in a ward of a State Mental Hospital." *The Little Foxes, Who's Afraid of Virginia Woolf?,* and *Les Liaisons Dangereuses* all take place in living rooms. Harold Pinter has said that when he starts to write a play, he imagines a room with a couple of people in it and someone comes in.

These contexts enable the play to look carefully at the human themes, to reveal what's in the human heart, whether it be the tyranny of Nurse Ratched, Regina's malice and cruelty, or Valmont's unexpected capacity to love. This philosophical and thematic focus of the theatre emphasizes the element that best conveys ideas while revealing character—language.

THEATRICAL DIALOGUE:
EXPLORING IDEAS

Film is a medium of images. It doesn't need a great deal of dialogue to move the story or to reveal character. In theatre, however, language is a key element, a means to explore ideas. The dialogue reveals humanity. Dialogue uses rhythms, a turn of phrase, a particularly well-chosen word to convey subtext. It focuses on the interplay of theme, character, subtext, and language, rather than on the story.

When a play is well written, even a bad actor looks good, almost as if the power of the language ennobles the actor. I was once told that Tennessee Williams's dialogue was so good that it could be read like a telephone book and it would still sound beautiful. I have seen two productions of Williams's plays done by mediocre actors who gave their best performances because of the strength of his words. In college, I performed one of my best scenes from the Tennessee Williams play *Something Unspoken* (and I was a "C" actor in almost all my other acting work).

In theatre it's not unusual to see a long speech of a page or more. Many of the most memorable lines in theatre come from long monologues. In film, that can be deadly. It can slow down the movement, interrupt relationships, and misplace the emphasis of a scene.

Film depends on much more than dialogue and the actor to make it work. Film is the director's medium, dependent upon the images and contexts that surround the actor. Theatre is the writer's and actor's medium, where great dialogue makes visible what is invisible, revealing important ideas and creating strong characters.

Great theatre, like the great novel, tends to be thematic and idea-oriented. In a novel, words are used to describe, reflect, and explain meanings and significance. A play puts these words into dialogue as it explores the ideas. Dialogue becomes an exchange between the actor and the audience. In *The Empty Space* Peter Brook says:

> A word does not start as a word—it is an end product which begins as an impulse, stimulated by attitude and behavior which dictate the need for expression. This process occurs inside the dramatist; it is repeated inside the actor. Both may only be conscious of the words, but both for the author and then for the actor the word is a small visible portion of a gigantic unseen formation. . . .

Dialogue contains subtext, hidden meanings that are revealed through the vehicle of the actor. Brook goes on to say, "The vehicle of drama is flesh and blood and here completely different laws are at work. The vehicle and the message cannot be separated."

This of course makes theatre more character-oriented than story-oriented. It puts the emphasis on the dialogue and the interrelationships between characters. This language of theatre is not just about talk, but about revelation; it's not about a message, it's about characters revealing the truth about humanity. It's not about somebody standing up and lecturing and telling us, it's about human meanings and human feelings.

Not just dialogue, however, reveals the human condition, but also the language of sound, the rhythms of the word, the texture of the words, the sounds in themselves.

In many of the absurdist playwright Eugene Ionesco's plays, language is used to confuse communication, rather than help it. In one of my favorite plays, Ionesco's *The Leader*, one character says the words, "Let's go to the market and get some eggs." The other character replies, "Oh, I love them as much as you do."

When I directed the play during college, one of my teachers helped me to understand some of the underlying meanings of Ionesco's nonsense words. In this case, the meaning of the first character's lines was explained to me as "Let's go make babies"—a rather unusual way to communicate that desire.

Occasionally there have been plays where the actors speak in abstract sounds that signify what is happening internally. In Ionesco's play *The Chairs* the actors have moved from dialogue to sound, ending the play with these "words":

ORATOR:
Mmm, Mmm, Gueue, Gou, Gu, Mmm, Mmm, Mmm, Mmm.

In many of these absurdist plays sound signifies the vain search for communication, the emptiness of our lives, the superficialities of relationships in which we never truly reach each other. Sometimes the message tells us that when we talk we say absurd things. The most essential communication is beyond words.

CHOOSING THE PLAY
TO ADAPT TO FILM

Clearly, much in theatre is untranslatable. Millions of dollars were spent trying to bring *A Chorus Line*, *Equus*, *Hair*, *Jesus Christ Superstar*, and *Godspell* to the screen, with little return on the investment. There are certain plays that seemed difficult to adapt, and yet the films worked beautifully, such as *Driving Miss Daisy* and *Amadeus*. What, then, do you look for?

Look for a play that can work in a realistic context. Even though *Children of a Lesser God* and *Amadeus* and *Driving Miss Daisy* used fluid, abstract sets, they implied real rooms and cars and carriages and concert halls. Nothing was lost by creating a realistic world.

Look for a play that can be opened up. *The Little Foxes* is set in a living room, but offstage characters go upstairs, travel on the train, live next door, and work down the street. In the film it was easy to include actual scenes showing these implied scenes. The play *Steel Magnolias* took place in a beauty parlor, but for the film it wasn't difficult to add bedrooms, living rooms, an outdoor reception, and a county fair, since the dialogue referred to action that took place in other spaces.

Look for a play that implies a story line. Some plays have little story, but when the play is converted to film, the story will need to come to the forefront. The play *Les Liaisons Dangereuses* was very stylized, placing its emphasis on subtext and dialogue. The film placed the emphasis on the story. In this play there was a story line that could be strengthened to help create a successful film. In the case of *A Chorus Line*, however, there wasn't.

Make sure that the play does not achieve its magic through its unique use of theatrical space. The sets of *Man of La Mancha*, *Godspell*, *Equus*, and *Hair* were an intrinsic part of the success of the plays, but that context could not translate into film. The way the abstract theatre space engaged the audience is what made these plays work. As soon as the settings became realistic, they lost an essential ingredient. I, for one, refused to see the film of *Equus* because I had no desire to see real horses blinded, and as soon as that scene was acted out realistically, it lost the symbolic meaning that made the play work in the theatre.

Find the play where the human themes can be expressed through cinematic images rather than through language. Many good plays rely on the richness of the spoken word. But film is essentially visual. If you can't see the play in motion, it may not be workable.

And if the play worked because of the special energy that comes from the audience-and-actor interaction, reconsider trying to adapt. Watching a film is not the same as watching a play. The energy of the theatrical experience can cover many flaws.

There have been many more failures in the translation of theatre to film than successes. At first glance.it seems as if plays are the closest to film and are naturals for adaptation. Yet the play is not the thing, it's the experience. The essential magic that creates theatre can't be translated; but with the right play, new magic can be created for film.

Perhaps Shakespeare best described the transitoriness and magic of theatre in *The Tempest* (Act IV, Scene i):

> *Our revels now have ended. These our actors,*
> *As I foretold you, were all spirits and*
> *Are melted into air, into thin air;*
> *And, like the baseless fabric of this vision,*
> *The cloud-capp'd towers, the gorgeous palaces,*
> *The solemn temples, the great globe itself,*
> *Yea, all which it inherit, shall dissolve;*
> *And, like this insubstantial pageant faded,*
> *Leave not a rack behind. We are such stuff*
> *As dreams are made on, and our little life*
> *Is rounded with a sleep.*

CASE STUDY:
Driving Miss Daisy

Driving Miss Daisy began as a play in the seventy-four-seat Off-Broadway theatre Playwrights Horizons in New York and later moved to the John Houseman Theatre.

Playwright and screenwriter Alfred Uhry charts the course of the play as it moved from the theatre to film. "To start with, about the third week of the run in this small theatre I was approached about shooting the play, just as it was, for television. Then the next week I was offered a cable television deal, and the next week, Angela Lansbury wanted to do a Movie of the Week. Then several different movie companies became interested in it. Originally Rob Reiner, Sam Goldwyn, and the Zanucks were interested. I eventually went with Zanuck and Brown, because their record was so extraordinary, and they had made so many pictures that I admired. I told them that I'd rather have no movie at all than have it be wrong, and that's why I wanted to try and write it. By wrong, I meant the wrong accents, the wrong words. In this delicate play, much of it has to be unsaid for it to work.

"Dick Zanuck found out that [director] Bruce Beresford was available, and in twenty-four hours, I was sitting with Bruce Beresford, and he chose, out of all his many projects, to do ours.

"At first, the studios all wanted it and then, all of a sudden, nobody wanted it, which was fine. I wasn't surprised. I never thought anybody would want it in the first place—a play about an old lady and an old man. But they said, it's beautiful and it's wonderful, and nobody will go see it. Finally Warner Brothers financed about five-sevenths of it and Jake Ebert in London financed the rest of it. The cost of the picture was seven and a half million dollars and it was shot in forty-six days.

"When you write for the stage, you have to tell people a lot of things, but in a movie you can show them everything. You can be much more subtle in a movie than in a play. You can say much less and show much more.

"The film is different from the play because it's more populated. In the play, Hoke sits on a stool and pretends to drive a car. However, the play implies all the realistic sets.

"The play was not abstract, which helped the adaptation. It contained twenty-six short scenes which were almost cinematic. When I wrote the play, I was aware of this cinematic action. I saw my work for the film as filling in the scenery, filling in the blanks, and filling in the colors. I didn't want to change the focus, and I didn't.

"I thought a movie with three people in it would be mo-notonous, so I made a rule for myself that I would bring in all the people I talked about in the play and no more. I brought in Florine, the wife of Boolie, Idella the maid, Uncle Walter's birthday party with the whole family, and the people that were there when Boolie gets his award. I wanted to keep the focus where it was, and I didn't want to make up any subplots. I've seen plays adapted for the screen where they put in subplots which weigh it down. I thought of it as focusing on two and a half people, Miss Daisy, Hoke, plus the smaller role of the son.

"I cut any dialogue that I could show rather than tell about. I found that some things in the play were repetitive. In a movie you can say much less and show much more. I kept the dia-logue at a minimum, while trying to re-create the way that people talk. When adapting your own work you have to be ruthless about making it into a movie. You can't fall in love with the sound of your words. You have to see it as a film and not just as some actors saying your words. A good actor in a movie has to say about a third of what a good actor has to say on the stage. So much of what they say is subtext. People like Hoke and Miss Daisy who have an ongoing relationship gen-erally say the same things, yet I still needed to pick interesting things for them to say. I wanted to keep the dialogue at a min-imum, while still re-creating the way that people talk.

"Morgan Freeman added some dialogue, since he had created the part in the play. And he's exactly my age and also from the South, so there were certain words that he remembered, such as 'chifferobe,' which is a Southern word for bureau. Jessica played it exactly as written.

"Adapting is a bit like redecorating. You have to rethink the script. Why is this a movie? It's a movie because it's fluid, it moves around. I was excited about really recreating the Atlanta of my childhood. I could describe the way the neighborhood looked, that remarkable house, and real cars.

"Some of the characters needed some rethinking. Lili Zanuck was convinced in a draft that Florine was turning out to be a bitch, and I said, 'I don't mean her to be a bitch. I just mean her to be a flirtatious person.' When Lili made that comment, I went back and reexamined her.

"After Jessica had agreed to play the part of Miss Daisy, Dick Zanuck said, 'There's got to be somewhere where Jessica can smile. She seems so grim all the time, and Jessica's got the most beautiful smile in the world.' We added the smile at the birthday party when her older brother cuts the cake and she gives that picture perfect, wonderful smile.

"Much of my work was cutting. There are cuts in almost every single scene. Bruce was helpful in this regard. We would look at a speech, and he could see what we could lose.

"Some of the work meant adding to the play. Since Bruce is Australian, he didn't know much about the South. He would ask me, 'Tell me what you remember about your childhood that you think is interesting.' That conversation resulted in a scene that isn't in the play, a scene without dialogue when Hoke serves Daisy her dinner and then goes back in the kitchen and eats his own dinner off a different plate with different cutlery.

"I also added a scene with two policemen. I wanted them in the play, but we weren't able to hire two actors to have bit parts in the play. But I could bring them into the film.

"Audiences seem to identify with the film. Often people comment on the film or play by saying 'You must have known my mother,' or 'You must have known my Uncle Joe.' It seems to me that my family must have been like a lot of people's families."

Driving Miss Daisy was nominated for eight Academy Awards and won four, for Best Picture, Best Screenplay Adaptation, Best Actress, and Best Makeup. This small film, which many producers and studios said no one would go to see, has now made well over one hundred million dollars.

WHY THE TRUE-LIFE
STORY RESISTS FILM

When I was a girl growing up in a small town in northern Wisconsin, reading biographies and autobiographies of famous people expanded my horizons and taught me valuable human lessons. From Clara Barton I learned about strength and determination; Jane Addams taught me about compassion; and Amelia Earhart taught me that it was all right to be different. As I grew older I learned about introspection and a very private spirituality through Dag Hammarskjöld, about dignity and justice through Martin Luther King, Jr., and about overcoming overwhelming odds through the story of Sir John Hunt's expedition to Mount Everest.

Biographies took me around the world to places I never expected to visit. They introduced me to people I would never meet. Biographies also explored the inner lives of people unlike myself. They took me into the subjective world of different experiences, attitudes, feelings, and perspectives. Other people's inner lives are rarely accessible to us, except for those of our very best friends. Rarely do we have the privilege of learning what it's like to be someone else, to see the world through someone's else's eyes—for instance, what it means to be of another race (*Black Like Me* by John Griffin, or *The Autobiography of Malcolm X*), or of another religion (*The Diary of Anne Frank*); or what it means to have a disability (*My Left Foot*).

The subjects of true-life stores can move us with their courage. They can point the way, by helping us explore careers, relationships, other realities. They can teach us values as well as issue a warning about dangers and the consequences of certain behavior. They can take us into dark worlds, educating us about corruption and injustice, manipulation and victimization, wasted and decadent lives.

A good biography can take us inside the heart of its subject. Listen to how Christy Brown describes the moment when he realized he was different.

> I was now just ten, a boy who couldn't walk, speak, feed or dress himself. I was helpless, but only now did I begin to realise how helpless I really was. I still didn't know anything about myself: I knew nothing beyond the fact that I was different from others. I didn't understand what made me different or why it should be. I just knew that I couldn't run about, or play football, or climb trees, or even feed myself as the others did. I couldn't reason this out. I couldn't even think clearly about it. I could only feel it, feel it deep down in the very core of me, like a thin sharp needle that worked its way through all the fancies and dreams of my childish mind till it tore them to shreds, leaving it naked and powerless to avoid the stark reality, that I was a cripple.

Later he writes:

> I could now no longer run away from myself, I had grown too big for that. In a thousand ways, large and small, as each day went by, as the family grew up one by one and became—to me—strange self-supporting adults, I saw and felt the limitations, the boredom, the terrible narrowness of my own existence. All around me

were signs of activity, effort, growth. Everyone had something to do, something to occupy them and keep their minds and their hands active. They had interests, activities and aims to make their lives an integrated whole and give their energies a natural outlet and a natural medium of expression. I had only my left foot.

Through these words we share Christy's struggle. This is the book's strength. But this kind of material does not translate well into film. Biography resists the objectivity of film. If all you have with biography is a rich inner life, it will be a difficult, perhaps an impossible, adaptation. The screenwriters of *My Left Foot* certainly saw that problem and approached this very subjective material by not following the book at all. By drawing on other material besides the book and combining and changing characters and situations, they created a film.

CHOOSING A WORKABLE STORY LINE

Film is a story medium. Aristotle told us that drama is about "one action," one consistent story line. Clearly he wasn't thinking of the true-life story. There are many stories within one life; a life defies cinematic neatness and creates difficulties for anyone choosing which story to show. If you're doing a film on Martin Luther King, Jr., for instance, are you going to tell his whole life story or only emphasize his part in the civil rights movement? Are you going to focus on his relationship with Coretta Scott King? Or perhaps it should be the story of the theological journey that led him to make a number of decisions about the relationship of religion and social action? What are you going to do about some of the negative stories we've heard about this man: the affairs, or possibly even the alleged plagiarism that has come to light recently? What's going to be your take on King? Which of the stories has a clear beginning, middle, and end? Of course, in the case of Martin Luther King, Jr., we know him for his work with the civil rights movement, so we can see some center around which we could fashion a story.

Which story would you tell if you were going to write about John Glenn? Or Clare Booth Luce? Or Elizabeth Taylor? How would you focus the material if you had to write about playwright Eugene O'Neill or songwriter Stephen Foster?

Many of these stories do not have clear beginnings, middles, and ends. Sometimes one theme in somebody's life doesn't end until the person dies, and another theme ends when the subject is twelve. Sometimes stories have no real development. A woman decides that she wants to become an actor, she goes to her first casting call, she is cast immediately. There's no struggle, there's no development, no conflict. She's just plain lucky. How are you going to tell her story?

Everybody is a combination of many stories; some begin and end early, some begin and end late, and some of them continue through sixty or seventy years of life. Some extremely important stories might be very, very short. Some parts of a life are epic, some episodic, some are short-term story lines but very important in contributing to the meaning of a person's life.

CREATING DRAMATIC ORDER

Not only are there many stories in one person's life, but seldom does anyone live his or her life in the right dramatic order. Instead of the stories building to one neat dramatic climax, the climax to one subplot might occur far later than the climax of the A, or main, story line. Some characters make one appearance and never appear again. And there are always some people who are an integral part of a person's life but have nothing to do with the particular story you're trying to tell.

As a script consultant, I have worked with many true-life stories. In one case, I helped a producer evaluate the feasibility of a television movie about a country-western singer. Unfortunately, the climax of his career, winning a major country-western award, came before his subplot love story. There was no major conflict. And there was no relationship subplot that continued for a significant portion of his life. Although more research might have yielded a strong dramatic story line, further thinking about the project showed us that the investment of time and money probably was not worth it.

A few years ago I was called in on a project about a famous musician. I met with him and the producer to try to find a possible story line. After some discussion I discovered there was a strong dramatic story line in his rise to fame, culminating with his work with Louis Armstrong. When I outlined the possibility, he immediately countered, "But that doesn't include when I used to dance and sing with the radio when I was four, or my visit to Berlin last year." Although this could have been a viable and important story, the inability to focus the material led to its abandonment.

The specific details of true-life stories often get in the way of creating a strong dramatic through-line. In 1989 I was hired by the Mormon church to work on a film about the Mormons' epic journey from New York State to the area that became Salt Lake City in the middle eighteen hundreds. Since the church insists on everything being factual and has a staff of researchers, there was no room for dramatic license. On one occasion I asked Kieth Merrill, the director (and original writer), if we could shift the location of a certain speech to the east side of the river because it would make a stronger dramatic build for a particular sequence. He called Salt Lake City and reported back that since the speech took place on the west side of the river, we'd have to rework the sequence to be factual. He made several similar calls to Salt Lake with the same result. In this case, however, the work led to a successful result, and the film (*Legacy*) is now being shown in Salt Lake City as part of a historical introduction to the Mormons.

THE TRUE-LIFE INCIDENT

It is usually easier to adapt a true-life incident than a true-life story because the material often contains a rising dramatic line leading to a strong climax. Examples of true-life incidents are films that focus on one major event in someone's life, rather than on an ongoing story line that may cover a number of years and a number of subplots. For instance, the television movie of *Everybody's Baby: The Rescue of Jessica McClure* takes place over a three-day period. It contains a climax (her rescue) and the drama and suspense building up to it. The Karen Silkwood story takes place over a number of months, but also focuses specifically on the drama and suspense of Karen's discovery of problems at the Kerr-McGee plant. *The Burning Bed* is built around an incident of murder and abuse. *Murder in Mississippi* is built around the murder of three civil rights workers. All of these stories are implicitly dramatic. No one has to look very far to see where the drama is, and to see a definite structure within the material that sets up the incident, develops it, and then ends the story with a strong climax. This doesn't mean that the writer does not need to find artistic and original ways of ordering the material, but the writer can begin the process, knowing that the drama is there.

The true-life epic demands much more detective work. What event, out of an entire lifetime, will be the focus of the drama? How do you keep a true-life story from becoming episodic? Clearly it is impossible to tell the "womb to tomb" story in two hours. Even if you could tell it, the story would be unfocused and unconnected and would not add up to compelling drama.

WHAT DO YOU LOOK FOR?

Some true-life stories are easy to adapt. If you see the following elements, you know there's a reasonable chance of creating a successful film:

1. A central incident that can help focus your subject. Even a true-life epic story like the story of Gandhi focused on his work to create change nonviolently in India. If the story centers on one event that is objective and external, you should be able to build a dramatic, focused story line. *Separate but Equal, Crossing to Freedom, Friendly Fire,* and *The Murder of Mary Phagan* all have an implicit focus in their stories.

2. A story building to a clear climax. The story of the civil rights murders implies two possible climaxes, depending on whether you start with the murder of the civil rights workers, as in *Mississippi Burning,* or end with the murder, as in the television film *Murder in Mississippi.* By starting with the murder the film version built to a climax that showed the arrest and conviction of the murderers. By ending with the murder, the television version focused on the work of the civil rights workers, building to their deaths as a consequence of their work. Clearly there was inherently dramatic material within this incident.

3. Sympathetic main characters. Do we like the characters? Are they fascinating? Do we want to spend time in their company? Most true-life stories will center on compelling characters who have made some contribution to the world. Examples of these would be movies about George Washington, the Kennedys, Eleanor and Franklin Roosevelt, or Annie Sullivan and Helen Keller in *The Miracle Worker.* Some true-life stories, such as *The Burning Bed, Killing in a Small Town, Roe vs. Wade,* or *Playing for Time,* present us with subjects who are in a difficult situation. The film gives us insights and also awakens our compassion and understanding.

This does not mean that the antihero can never work in an adaptation. The success of *GoodFellas,* based on the true story of Henry Hill, shows that a glimpse into the life-style of an immoral character can make a compelling film. But examples of this are rare. Before you attempt this kind of story, it's important to recognize the potential for alienating audiences or finding that people don't want to see your film because they don't like your characters.

4. A story that covers a short period of time. The shorter the time the story covers, the easier it will be to keep the story focused. The three-day period that Jessica spent in the well will implicitly be easier to deal with than the life of Karen Blixen (*Out of Africa*). The Montgomery, Alabama, bus boycott (as in *The Long Walk Home*) will be easier to deal with than the entire civil rights movement.

5. Strong ongoing relationships between at least two characters. Drama is about relationship. People rarely go through life by themselves. If your subject spends most of his or her life alone, you will have considerable difficulty creating a dramatic, dynamic story line. If at least one relationship within the story has a strong conflict, perhaps between a protagonist and an antagonist, more drama will emerge. The antagonist can be a group, such as the law enforcement authorities in the TV movies *Adam* and *M.A.D.D.*, or the whole welfare system, as in *The Burning Bed*, provided these group antagonists are actual people who represent the larger group, not abstract ideas. To get strong drama there needs to be some opposition.

If the story also has an ongoing love relationship of some kind, this will give your character a confidante and give you further opportunity to dimensionalize the characters through a positive relationship. Think about the texture and dimensionality we saw in Karen Silkwood through her relationship with her boyfriend, or in Eric in *Chariots of Fire* through his relationship with his sister, or in Lieutenant Dunbar in *Dances With Wolves* through his relationship with Stands With A Fist.

6. A story that can be told visually. Climbing Mount Everest is visual. Someone writing the all-American novel is not. Capturing drug dealers is visual. A story of Wolfgang Puck creating new recipes may not be.

7. A rising dramatic line, rather than repetitive action. Stories that build to a great moment will be easier to translate than stories that are repetitious. Winning at the Olympics will be an easier story to tell than the story of a young ballerina practicing

every day and finally getting a small part in *The Nutcracker*. Some films will use montages to move quickly through repetitive elements. This has worked well with many Rocky-type underdog triumph stories. But it doesn't work as well with stories that are about practicing, rehearsing, preparing, or doing any of the same actions over and over again. The most dramatic stories will be those that build in tension, excitement, and/or intensity.

BE CAREFUL

Material that is dependent on a great deal of backstory information can cause a number of translation problems. Generally backstory information needs to be communicated through flashbacks and exposition. Both of these techniques can work against the drama of the story. The more there is to communicate, the more back-heavy the story will be, and the more the story will continually look back to the information we need to know, rather than forward to the unfolding of the story.

Material that is internal and psychological, that concentrates on inner thoughts and motivations, will be difficult to express dramatically. Many letters and diaries are about thoughts rather than actions. Although they can reveal fascinating characters, they may not contain a usable storyline.

If too much time elapses in the course of the story the translation can be difficult. Epics are, by their very nature, the most difficult to adapt because the longer the period of time, the easier it is for the drama and focus to be dissipated. When too much time has elapsed in a story, it becomes difficult to bridge events. Transitions from one year to another are essentially nondramatic, and usually consist of words across the screen such as FIVE YEARS LATER. If we're seeing only events that are far apart in time, we begin to lose their relationship and the story becomes episodic, rather than developmental.

Be careful of material with no inherent conflict, and no antagonist. If no one opposes the subject of your story, there will be no relationship, no conflict, no drama.

Be careful of material where your main subject is his or her own worst enemy. If the subject causes his or her own problems, we may lose sympathy.

Be careful of subjects who have too much good luck. If all their goals are easy, with no obstacles in the way, it will be difficult for the audience to identify with them and to root for them.

Be careful of subjects who have moved around a great deal over the years and have no ongoing relationships. If every ten minutes new characters come into their lives, it will be difficult to develop any subplots and any continuing relationships. People who are part of someone's true-life story for only a short period of time can be confusing to audiences, resulting in "scenes from a life" rather than a cohesive story line.

This is not to say that these subjects must never be attempted. There are many examples of adaptations that have done well in spite of the difficulties I've mentioned, but they've done well because of the writer's ability to analyze the problems clearly and to create original solutions. When these problems are inherent in the material, you must think about it very carefully before plunging in.

Great writers have found creative solutions to seemingly impossible translations. The true-life stories of Emile Zola, Florenz Ziegfield, General Patton, Gandhi, Karen Blixen, and the last emperor of China all won Academy Awards. The biographies of Eleanor and Franklin, King Edward and Mrs. Simpson, Golda Meir, Peter the Great, and the story of Roe vs. Wade all won Emmy Awards. These successes show that a true-life story, well done, has the potential to involve, fascinate, and inspire us.

CASE STUDY:
Reversal of Fortune

In 1990 there were a number of great true-life adaptations, including *Dances With Wolves*, written and adapted by Michael Blake, *Awakenings*, adapted by Steven Zaillian, and *Reversal of*

Fortune, adapted by Nicholas Kazan. I have great affection for all three of these films.

I admired Michael Blake's ability to create a three-hour film that felt like two hours. This success did not come just from the directing. Much depended on his ability to pace and structure the material.

I was touched by *Awakenings* and cared deeply about the people in this film. I admired Steven Zaillian's ability to take a simple theme about awakening to life and make it resonate on many different levels.

And I was fascinated by *Reversal of Fortune*, the story of the Claus von Bulow appeal. There were a number of problems implicit in the material, which took smart writing, smart directing, and smart casting to overcome. This was a film that shouldn't have worked—it had so many elements working against it. Yet by carefully thinking through the problems and creatively solving them, Nicholas Kazan was able to create a workable and intriguing script. Nicholas discusses his approach to the script.

"This was one of the most difficult scripts I've written. There were times when I thought there was so much material, so many details in the legal case, so much information to cram into a film, and so many stories to tell, that at first I didn't know how to do it. I had the transcripts of the two trials to work from, the two-thousand-plus-page depositions of Claus's testimony in the civil-suit trial [which is the only place where Claus ever gave his version of the story], and I also had the depositions which he gave to the police, which were much more circumspect, to say the least. Evasive.

"The story was also difficult because it's about an appeal. And an appeal is based on a trial where the defendant has already been convicted. A trial is a very dramatic event, and most legal films are properly about trials. You lead toward the trial. The trial happens at the end. You render the verdict and then there's the aftermath and the end of the movie. But an appeal is made up of one hundred seventeen pieces of paper, collated and bound together and added to a judgment. Then a couple of months later we get to hear the lawyers of each side talk to the judges for half an hour and answer questions, and then months later, there's a verdict. It's completely antidramatic.

"I saw the structure of this film as unconventional. True, there's a beginning, middle, and an end, but in a sense, this story began in the middle with the appeal. When I started working, I first came up with the final scene of the movie where he goes into the drugstore. I told it to Ed Pressman [the producer] and he laughed.

"I also knew I had to summarize the case for the audience. But the problem is that part of the audience for the film knew a great deal about the case, part of the audience knew a little bit about the case, and part of the audience knew nothing about the case. So I had to summarize the case in a way that would not bore the people who already knew a lot about it. The only way I could see to do that was to have Sunny summarize the case, because no one had heard that viewpoint before.

"Once I made that decision, that fractured the film for me. It meant that it had to be in certain sections. If I started with Sunny, and then she introduces Dershowitz, and then Dershowitz talks about Claus . . . then the structure was free. I knew I had to have flashbacks, because I had to hear Claus's version of the events.

"At the end of the film, Sunny says that 'that's all you can know, all you can be told, when you get where I am you'll learn the rest.' And I realized that that's what's exciting about any murder case, you don't ever really know all the answers for sure.

"I see the critical element of any story as having a sense of mystery, wanting to know what's going to happen next. In this case I had to have as many little mysteries as I could have. Who is Alan? Who is this woman? Is she really his girlfriend? Will they knock out the medical testimony? Can we discredit their witnesses? Is Claus really guilty? Early on, Alan says that he wants to find out who Claus really is. I have him say that so the audience will also say, 'Yeah, I want to find out who this guy is.' All these dramatic questions are sprinkled throughout as a way of sustaining the mystery throughout the film.

"I realized that if I was going to add Sunny in a coma to the beginning and the end, I had to have her in the middle or the audience would forget her. I could work other elements into these scenes. Sunny could talk honestly about her drug addiction. By cutting back to the body periodically, I could remind the audience that this woman's life is essentially over. Here's a life that's ended.

"My analogy for the film was juggling. I had to throw balls up in the air, and then one would come down, and then I'd throw a couple more up, and try to keep as many balls up in the air as possible so that you were constantly saying, 'Oh yeah, what about that? And what about that?' So I had this sense of all these things happening at once the way it really was because they had to discredit all the aspects of the case in order to have a chance at the appeal.

"There is a kind of structure, but the structure is based on the mystery of the questions. I knew that Claus's story about the first coma and the second coma were going to be very satisfying to the audience. I also knew that Claus's story of the second coma didn't completely answer all the questions, so there were other issues that needed to be raised. So I put the first coma about halfway through the film, and the second coma toward the end. I had all these issues—Did Sunny try to kill herself? Why didn't Claus call the doctor? Why was Sunny's nightgown hiked up? etc.—so I spaced them out for impact so that as you went through the film, you felt like you were learning more and more about the case. You were learning that Claus seemed to be innocent of injecting her with insulin, but perhaps there were other questions that also had to be addressed.

"The film is billed as a comedy, and it obviously has a comic dimension. In fact, both Claus and Alan are extremely funny. Although I wasn't allowed to meet Claus [because of a civil suit that restrained him from publicizing the case], there was a certain ironic tone that I extrapolated from the material. I knew I was writing extravagant characters. Some of the scenes with Claus and Sunny show this comedy. If you give people a good electric character with a good electric charge, and you have them rub up against each other, some of the interrubbing is going to have a comic dimension.

"Some of the first lines of the film were meant to have a comic dimension. At the beginning, Sunny says, 'Brain dead, body better than ever.' I hoped people would laugh at it. I originally also had a line when Sunny said she was a vegetable, perhaps a brussels sprout. And there was a subtle line when she describes Alexandra Aisles, 'Claus's mistress, the very beautiful Alexandra,' and you know from the way she says 'beautiful' that she hates her.

"Portraying the characters presented certain problems. The character of Claus is fascinating because he's constantly flirting with people's expectation and image of him that he's this horrible human being. He seems to relish the fact that he's seen in this way. It's kind of a bizarre trait, but it's certainly tantalizing and makes you constantly go back and forth between liking him and disliking him, being intrigued by him, laughing with him, laughing at him, being alarmed by what he says. It's a very three-dimensional portrait.

"Alan Dershowitz, though, is really the protagonist of the film. He's the active character. He's the one that is seeking the truth, trying to reverse the conviction. But Dershowitz is always moving within the landscape of von Bulow, so it's as if everything around him, every prop, should reek of von Bulow. Claus is the more intriguing character because he's fascinating, ambivalent, ambiguous.

"As a main character, Alan Dershowitz is, in real life, like Woody Allen. But if I portrayed him realistically, everyone would say, 'He's too much like Woody Allen. We've seen that character on film, and it's Woody Allen, and I don't know why you're copying.' The fact that he is that way and grew up in the same part of Brooklyn as Woody Allen and came from the same tradition where they tell jokes and stories all the time didn't help, so I had to diminish that aspect of him.

"This was difficult, since Alan is a real living breathing person. And he's someone that I greatly respect, so I had a kind of quandary. I didn't want to portray him as a goody-two-shoes, since that gets boring. If I made up flaws, such as giving him a drinking problem, Alan would have grounds to sue me, since it's inaccurate. I finally made him grouchy and someone who lost his temper. Alan didn't like that, since he says he never loses his temper, but it was one of the few things that I could do that made him look more human so the audience would have more points of identification with him.

"It was also difficult getting the audience to sympathize with a lawyer hired to reverse the conviction of a man that most people assume is horrible and guilty. Audiences are accustomed to having a rootin' interest in their main character. Whatever the main character wants, they want. But in this case it wasn't quite so simple because Claus may be a murderer, so if Alan says, 'Let's get him off,' the audience will say, 'I don't want to get him off.' I needed to deal with these concerns very directly and very early. That's the reason for the long scene in Alan's office when the team is assembling. He's explaining that even if Claus is guilty, the lawyer has an obligation to defend the democratic process because if that process is not clean and fair, then innocent people will be convicted. Alan sees himself as the defender of the constitution. In that service, he defends people whom the audience might not like. In this case, it becomes more ambiguous as you see the evidence unravel, since maybe Claus isn't guilty.

"I'm sure there were students who didn't want to work on the case for that reason, but this gave Alan a good chance to make his arguments to defend the process. I had to bring this argument up early so that the audience could get on Alan's side and be rootin' for him to succeed with the case.

"There were several tricks with the character of Sunny. There was a great preponderance of evidence in the deposition showing that Sunny abused drugs. She smoked three or four packs of cigarettes a day, took huge amounts of laxatives, had prescriptions for various drugs all over the city. I wanted to honestly portray her as a depressed, semisuicidal person. Prior to each of her comas, Claus's affair with Alexandra came to Sunny's attention. That certainly made it look as though she was trying to kill herself. On the other hand, I had no desire to paint Sunny as an unpleasant and depressed and horrible person. Sunny was someone with too much money and she had very little interaction with the world. She could buy everything that she wanted except happiness. I felt we needed a few scenes that were unexpected and that showed a side of Claus and Sunny when everything was wonderful so we could get a sense of what the promise of this relationship was.

"One of my first notes to myself was to destroy the rich with sympathy. From my observations, rich people can have a terrible problem. Everyone wants their money so they have to hide. As a result they're very far from the earth, very far from human roots, from their animal roots. I was seeking to contrast Claus, who was always perfectly dressed, with Dershowitz. The first time you see Dershowitz, he's playing basketball by himself. So you go from somebody who's cerebral, who doesn't live in his body, to someone who's out there playing basketball.

"I also had another theme in mind. This is going to sound pretentious, yet I think we all thirst for justice, but we only find it in the arms of God. Claus says he wants 'justice,' but we can never be sure. Maybe this means he's guilty and he wants to be acquitted. Alan really does want justice. He wants a pure legal system, but the system, because it's administered by human beings who are innately fallible, is always impure.

"And in the end, we don't know what happened. Only Sunny knows. Sunny's in God's arms. She has found her own justice. But she can't tell us what it is. All she can do is hint. Tantalize us with the mystery."

In 1991 the script was nominated for the Writers Guild Award, the Academy Award for Best Screenplay, and the Golden Globe, and won The L.A. Film Critics Association Award for Best Screenplay, the Boston Film Critics Award, the Pen Center U.S.A West award, and the NATO/ShoWest Writer of the Year Award.

4

FROM FILM INTO FILM

Film is powerful. It can move us to tears and laughter. Film images can haunt us through bad dreams. I still remember as a young girl being taken out of the theatre during a preview for *King Kong*. My mother didn't want me to have nightmares about the horrifying, howling gorilla. (In those days, films took a long time to reach Peshtigo, Wisconsin. In this case, the 1939 film didn't play until the early 1950's.)

Film characters concern us and pull us into their lives. It's not unusual for audience members to think about a character for weeks or months after seeing a movie. Often characters inspire us, leading us to make new decisions. We fall in love with films, watching some over and over and continually finding more meaning with each viewing.

Since film can have such an impact on us, it's not unusual for producers and executives to look to the remake as a potential source of new films. What was popular and moving for one group of people has the potential to speak in new ways to contemporary audiences.

The updating and reinterpreting of dramatic material is nothing new. Shakespeare has been updated innumerable times. The

Peter Brook production of *A Midsummer Night's Dream* placed the play in a circus atmosphere. *The Merchant of Venice* has been set in the eighteenth century. Every year there are Broadway revivals of classic plays with new interpretations, many of which are successful and bring new significance to the material. The remake and revival is a staple of the American stage. A high percentage of these productions succeed.

Most film remakes, however, fail or have only limited success. Why? If it worked once, why can't the best writers, directors, and actors make it work again? What are the inherent problems in the remake? When is a remake worth doing—and when should the original be left alone?

WHAT QUALIFIES AS A REMAKE?

There are a few major categories of film-to-film adaptations: remakes of American films; American versions of foreign, usually French, films; and short films expanded into feature films. Most remakes come from American films, a few being remakes of silent films, such as *Cleopatra* or *Ben-Hur* or *The Ten Commandments*. Many come from the best films of the 1930's and 1940's, such as *King Kong, Scarface, The Prisoner of Zenda, A Star Is Born, The Postman Always Rings Twice, Whatever Happened to Baby Jane, The Phantom of the Opera, Stella Dallas (Stella), A Man Called Joe (Always)*. The most successful adaptation of an earlier film was *Heaven Can Wait*, adapted from *Here Comes Mr. Jordan*.

In most of these situations, the original film is based on a novel or a play, so the remake becomes an adaptation of an adaptation. *Heaven Can Wait* is based on a play by Harry Segall; *The Postman Always Rings Twice* is based on a novel by James Cain; *Stella Dallas* is based on a novel by Olive Higgins Prouty. In some cases, the well-known adaptation is based on an earlier film: the Stella story was filmed in 1925, 1937 (the classic *Stella Dallas*), and most recently in 1989.

Among American remakes of French films, some of the most familiar are *Breathless, The Man Who Loved Women, Boudu Saved from Drowning* (*Down and Out in Beverly Hills*), *Le Cadeau* (*The Toy*), *Diabolique* (*Reflections of a Murder*), and *Cousin, Cousine* (*Cousins*).

Another type of remake is the short film expanded into the feature film. In the last few years an increase in the number of film programs in universities and professional schools has led to more interest in adapting short student films into feature films. Many young filmmakers begin with an intention to use their half-hour film as an entree into the film industry, and, if possible, to turn it into a two-hour film that they can write, produce, and/or direct. George Lucas got his start with his student film, *THX-1138*, which became his first full-length feature film. James Deardon directed and wrote a short film that became *Fatal Attraction*.

Remakes have also been made from other types of film. In at least one case, the remake (*Memphis Belle*) was based on a documentary.

Television has had no more success with remakes than the film industry. Although some TV remakes, such as *The Man in the Iron Mask* with Richard Chamberlain or *A Christmas Carol* with George C. Scott, have been quite wonderful, others have received poor ratings and/or negative reviews. Some of these include *Stagecoach, Indiscreet, Letter to Three Wives, Casablanca, The Sun Also Rises, Shadow of Doubt*, and *The Defiant Ones*.

If you're going to do a remake, what do you look for? Why are so many remakes failures? What elements seem to be part of successful remakes?

CONTEMPORARY SIGNIFICANCE

"Why do it?" is the most important question a producer can ask before attempting a remake. A remake needs to have contemporary significance. There needs to be some new resonance, some new meaning that the film brings to contemporary audiences. If we just wanted to see the same old story, we could rent the original. A lack of contemporary relevance has been the downfall of many remakes. *King Kong, Always,* and *Stella* all failed partly because of their inability to contemporarize the originals.

The original of *Stella Dallas* resonated within the context of the 1930's. In this story, we see a lower-class woman married to a rich man, but unable to adjust her common behavior to the refinement of the upper class. Finally she leaves him. Later she arranges for her much loved daughter to live with the father, outwardly rejecting the daughter in order to give her more opportunities.

In the period of the 1930's the movie worked. At that time divorce was a stigma, and class was an issue. In a limited social context, the sacrifice of the mother was understandable. It made sense.

In a more contemporary social setting, however, the upper-class characters who can't accept the common and flamboyant Stella seem snobbish and shallow. The daughter's wishes are not taken into consideration. At the end of the film, the mother's sacrifice seems unnecessary, unwise. Both the mother and the child lose, and seemingly for no good reason.

At the height of the women's movement, an updated *King Kong* cast Jessica Lange as a breathless, blond bimbo starlet. *Cousins* was made at a time when traditional values were coming back to the forefront; it's about two cousins, both married, who become platonically and then sexually involved and leave their spouses. Today when there's little reason for men and women to stay in bad marriages, *Cousins* showed two people in repressive situations who would rather cheat on their spouses than resolve their problems—even if through divorce.

The 1978 film *Heaven Can Wait* did, on the other hand, successfully update the 1941 *Here Comes Mr. Jordan* by drawing on a number of popular contemporary social issues and movements: the antinuclear and environmental movements, the physical fitness craze, and the human-potential movement. The film introduced a problem with a polluting factory, it showed its main character working hard at getting his body in shape for the Superbowl, and there were strong themes of identity (who am I?), of social values (what are important contributions to society?) and enduring love.

CONTEXT

A successful remake updates the context. This is not as much of a problem with a period piece; many films set in the historical past such as *Ben-Hur*, *The Ten Commandments*, and some of the Frankenstein films, have worked well. But when a film is contemporarized, the context of the story changes. Sometimes it just doesn't work, no matter who does the remake.

The story of *A Man Called Joe* took place among the risky and dangerous atmosphere of World War II. In this story Pete (Spencer Tracy) is killed in a bombing raid but is told he needs to return to earth as the guardian angel for a new pilot, Ted. Much to Pete's chagrin, Ted becomes the love interest of his own girlfriend. Pete struggles with jealousy, and finally learns to let her go so she can get over her grief and get on with her life.

In the 1989 film *Always*, the context is the world of firefighting pilots in the western United States instead of the war. There are still dangers. The men still fly airplanes. Their work still demands courage. But many of the risks that seemed courageous and necessary in *A Man Called Joe* (flying too low in order to make a successful bomb run, for instance), seem foolhardy in *Always* (running out of fuel on a firefighting job or taking needless risks in what sometimes seems like false heroics). In the original, the risky secret reconnaissance missions that demanded the skill of the few crack pilots worked well. In the remake, a similar situation in a different context looks like bad management. The fires rage, but only one pilot is prepared to do his job.

In many foreign films, the context is not clear. Some begin in the middle of a story. *Cousin, Cousine* begins with a wedding. We don't know whose wedding. We don't know the names or relationships of most of the people. For some time we don't know who the main characters are. *Cousins* tried to solve some of these problems by clearly introducing the main characters at the beginning and giving us more information about the wedding. But it still didn't clearly define its context. We didn't know for some time that Maria was married to Tom, a womanizer, or that Larry was unhappy in his marriage to Tish. Without this information, the problem, the context, and the situation were not understandable.

THE STORY LINE

Like most adaptations, the most workable film remakes have strong story lines rather than an episodic structure. This partially explains the success of *Three Men and a Baby* (from *Three Men and a Cradle*) and the failure of *Cousins* or *The Man Who Loved Women*, or even *Stella*. Two thousand years ago Aristotle wrote, "Of all plots and actions the episodic are the worst. I call a plot episodic in which the episodes or acts succeed one another without probable or necessary sequence." A strong story line raises the level of audience involvement. But many foreign films are character- or theme-driven rather than plot-driven. Remakes based on an episodic film have rarely done well with American audiences.

Occasionally a remake has all the elements that should make it workable. In the case of the remake of *Narrow Margin*, good story decisions were carried through for two-thirds of the script, and then the story structure dissipated. It ultimately became an unsatisfying film. I had looked forward to this remake, since I particularly enjoy a good suspense thriller, and I'm a fan of both Gene Hackman and Anne Archer. I figured I couldn't go wrong.

The story has all the potential of a good film. The brief summary in Leonard Maltin's *TV Movies and Video Guide* of the 1952 film describes it as "a hard-boiled cop, transporting a gangster's widow against his will to the trial in which she'll testify, must dodge hit-men aboard their train who are trying to silence her." He goes on to describe the 1952 film as "fast-paced, well-acted, impressively shot in a claustrophobic setting."

On the particular day I saw the film, the theatre was filled. The audience's enjoyment was palpable for much of the film. The creative changes from the original to the remake seemed workable. The woman (Anne Archer) is no longer a gangster's widow, but a woman who has been on a blind date with a man who got killed. She witnessed the murder. Believing that no one knows she was in the room (including the murderers), she leaves town for her brother's cabin in northern Canada. The D.A. (Gene Hackman) discovers she was in the room, tracks her down, and then the chase starts, the two escaping on a train with the hit-men on their heels. The remake has a tight and interesting setup and potentially interesting development between these two people. There are delightful scenes on the train between the D.A. and a small boy who keeps thinking he is a train robber. For two-thirds of the film the audience was having a wonderful time. But by the end of the film, the audience gave a collective sigh of disappointment. The film had degenerated into cliché "chase on top of the train" scenes. The action became incredible as the D.A. (a man whose job is mainly a thinking, legal job) managed to kill off all the hit-men. Here was a film that should have worked. But it lost its structure and its story in the last third of the film—and never lived up to its implicit dramatic potential.

THE VALUE SYSTEM

Especially in adaptations of foreign films there needs to be some recognition that different cultures have different value systems. In spite of our sophistication, there is still a puritanical streak in the American consciousness. We tend to be more conservative, more repressive, and even today tend to be particularly uncomfortable with sexuality outside the monogamous, heterosexual

norm. Whereas foreign films might deal with adultery or homo-
sexuality without making any value judgments, these are not
acceptable life-styles to many Americans.

When Americans focus on a triangle, the mistress (or the
man) usually must pay a price or a lesson must be learned (as
in *Fatal Attraction*). In American films, family values and mo-
nogamy usually emerge as the prevalent values. This is not
necessarily true in other cultures. Many remakes, particularly
of French films, put an emphasis on adulterous relationships and
womanizing. Films such as *Cousins*, *The Man Who Loved Women*,
and *Reflections of a Murder* treat mistresses and/or multiple sexual
relationships almost as a natural part of one's family.

If the values don't translate from one culture to another,
Americans will have trouble identifying with the life-styles or
morality of a film.

BE CREATIVE

As in any type of adaptation, staying too close to the original
film's story may actually work against the spirit of the story.
While researching this chapter I watched innumerable remakes
and was surprised at how closely they followed the original in
the structure, the story line, and even very small character details. For instance, in *Always*, Pete (Richard Dreyfuss) pulled at
his eyebrows in the same way Spencer Tracy did in the earlier
version. In *King Kong*, the natives of the island wore the same
costumes and took part in the same kind of ritual as in the earlier
version, in spite of the considerable amount of additional knowledge we now have of primitive cultures.

The best remakes were those where the writer was not afraid
to change the original. Many of the remakes strengthened the
story line. Even in some of the unsuccessful remakes, the film
worked best when story lines and character subplots were
strengthened. In *Cousins*, subplots were strengthened. In *Always*, the updated Ted was a more developed character than the
original Ted. There were a number of charming details added

to the characters of Pete and Dorinda that made them at least as likable as the originals.

In other remakes, such as *King Kong*, certain stylistic choices were interesting and potentially workable. Not until about half-way through the film did I realize that it was supposed to be funny. The ad on the back of the videotape confirmed that the film was meant to be camp. This might have worked if it had been properly set up and carried through. But the director and the actors didn't seem to understand the style. Aside from Jessica Lange, who was consistently playing her character as camp, most of the actors were very serious. Jeff Bridges played a straightforward hero. Charles Grodin played an obsessive scientist without a trace of humor. The opening scenes were played as a dark action-adventure. Without a clear camp style, much of the beginning of the film seemed merely stupid, silly, incredible. Yet as the movie proceeded, some of the lines were amusing. Dwan (Jessica Lange) calls King Kong a "chauvinist pig ape." Jack Prescott (Jeff Bridges) says, "Who the hell do you think went through there—some guy in an ape suit?"

Even if the style had worked, the film would still have lacked contemporary relevance. But imagine a production of *King Kong* now—with our current concerns about ecology and the extinction of rare species. If the camp style were used, imagine Madonna as the starlet who "won't take nothing from nobody," probably not even from a gorilla.

Adapting film into film takes as much thought as any other adaptation. If you are going to adapt a film you need to confront the same problems. Analyzing, evaluating, and solving those problems are the subjects of Part Two of this book.

CASE STUDY:
Fatal Attraction

The biggest box office hits that have been film remakes have been *Heaven Can Wait, Three Men and a Baby*, and *Fatal Attraction*, adapted by James Deardon. Since I believe student films may be an important future source of remakes, I called James Deardon in London, and we talked about the process of adapting his short film into the feature film *Fatal Attraction*.

"*Fatal Attraction* began in 1979 as a forty-five-minute film called *Diversions*. I produced, directed, and wrote it for GTO films as a short second feature, which was shown with the main feature. England was doing these kinds of films at this time as a way of encouraging young filmmakers. I made it on thirty-five millimeter, with a budget of fifty thousand dollars. Before this, I had made two previous short films—one was eight minutes long, the other was twenty minutes long.

"Sherry Lansing and Henry Jaffe had seen the film, and talked about doing a feature film with me. We threw a few ideas around, but we kept returning to this film, feeling that there was a feature-length film here.

"The short film covers the first weekend, and ends on the Monday after their affair. He stays the night, goes home, tries to cover his tracks, his wife returns from the country, and then the phone starts ringing. Just when you thought it was a great weekend, it becomes a nightmare. The short film was virtually the first act of the longer film. We compressed it to thirty minutes, since a forty-five-minute first act would be too long for a feature film. We had to add the party at the beginning, since in the short film they had already known each other.

"The basic mechanism of the plot was there in the short film. She keeps coming back and doesn't let him go. That was the motor of the short film and that became the motor of the feature.

"I had actually conceived the story as a long film. At the back of my mind, I had a number of ideas for extending it. I thought they might have met again at the beginning of the second act, perhaps five years later. He's divorced, whereas she's survived. Maybe she would have been much more in control.

"I could have taken the premise of a triangle and stretched it over ninety or one hundred minutes. I might have left out the cutting of her wrist at the end of the first act, and I could have played out the relationship over a much longer amount of time, focusing on an affair which could have culminated in all the kinds of pressures she would have brought to bear over a longer period of time.

"But since all this happened in the short film, and it worked, we made the short film the basic building block of the feature. Instead of stretching the short film, we said, 'Let's take this short film and make it into the first act.' That's why the film had a lot of energy. The irony is, we took the forty-five-minute film, added scenes, then condensed it into thirty minutes, so it became very dense. The film tended to grab you by the lapels in the first ten minutes and not let you go. The more traditional approach is to extend the story rather than condense it.

"We kept the story going by escalating her responses. It got outrageous, but I think it sort of holds together. It was an organic process to keep pushing the story—the kidnapping of Ellen, the killing of the rabbit.

"In the draft of the feature film, Dan actually goes to Alex's house to kill her. He makes elaborate preparations so they won't suspect him, but when he gets there, he can't bring himself to do it. He leaves, she commits suicide [which brings out the Madame Butterfly motif] and he gets blamed for it. It was a more subtle ending. After the film was tested with audiences, the ending got changed to the more fast-paced, commercial ending.

"In the short film, Dan was more the instigator. He had a little black book where he kept the names of other women, even though he was married. For the movie, he becomes a sympathetic character who is more revved up by her lunacy. He's less predatory, more vulnerable in the longer film. For a commercial film, you have to like your leading character and it has to have a happy ending. We had to make it more accessible to a wider public."

PART
TWO

CREATING
THE SECOND
ORIGINAL

FINDING THE STORY

Film and television are story mediums. Adapting is a process of identifying and focusing the story line within the novel, play, or true-life story. But this is no easy matter, since the story line is often hidden among character details, thematic statements, information and descriptions.

What is a good dramatic story? What elements are necessary to create a workable screenplay? What are you looking for when you're trying to extract a dramatic story line from all the other elements?

A good film story has *direction*. It moves toward a climax, with most scenes advancing the action. This movement keeps the audience involved as it anticipates what will happen next.

A good film story also has *dimensionality*. While the story is moving you, it is also revealing characters and developing themes. In my classes I draw the relationship between direction and dimensionality like this:

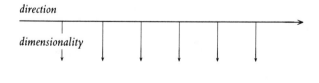

Sometimes these two elements are out of balance. Many foreign films concentrate on dimensionality but lack direction. Although they are often critically acclaimed for their insights, rarely are they commercially successful on the international market.

American films, however, often lack dimensionality. They become overloaded with action that overpowers their theme. Even action films need some dimensionality to work. They still need to be about something. They still need original characters to captivate and appeal to us.

A good story balances these two elements. In this chapter we'll look at only the action elements. The following three chapters will focus on bringing dimensionality to the action.

THE ELEMENTS OF A GOOD STORY

A story is a series of events or incidents that have a beginning, middle, and end. Aristotle said that a story is "one action." This means the events are related to each other. The writer selects and arranges a series of these incidents so they build with increasing intensity or suspense toward an exciting or dramatic resolution. By the end of the story, the events need to "add up," "make sense," and give the audience a feeling that it has arrived somewhere and completed the story's journey.

When adapting, the writer looks for the beginnings, middles, and ends within the original source material, and selects the events that create a strong, dramatic story line. Some story lines, however, are more workable than others. Therefore, the adaptor's work is fourfold: to identify, to evaluate, and, if necessary, to add to or to create story lines.

Look for a Goal

The easiest story lines are about a mission or achieving some goal. A character wants something—and goes after it. Sherlock

Holmes wants to solve a crime. Fred C. Dobbs in *The Treasure of the Sierra Madre* wants to find gold. The boys in *Stand by Me* want to find a dead body.

Goal-oriented story lines are the easiest to adapt because you can usually find the beginning, middle, and end of the story line by asking three questions: "What does the character want?" (when he or she gets it, that's the end of the story); "What does the character do to achieve the goal?" (middle of the story); and "When does the 'want' begin?" (the beginning of the story).

Detective stories and action-adventures tend to be easy adaptations because the goal is clear. A character comes to Perry Mason/Miss Marple/Sherlock Holmes/Hercule Poirot, etc. and asks for help (the want is established—the story has begun). The character accepts the job and begins investigating/discovering/finding out (this "doing" action makes up the middle of the story). The character then resolves the problem, usually after great threats to life and limb, culminating in a big shootout or an exciting capture (the end of the story).

Here we see a clear beginning, middle, and end to the story, and one action—"achieving the goal." You can see these goal-oriented story lines in many "incident-related" true-life stories. In *Everybody's Child* the goal is to get Jessica out of the well. In *Fatal Vision* the goal is to establish whether Dr. MacDonald is innocent or guilty. In *Killing in a Small Town*, the goal is to find out who did the crime and why.

If only finding the story lines were so clear and simple! Most stories won't be so neat. Not every story is about a goal. But there are other ways to find the story. Sometimes you can find it by defining the problem.

Look for a Problem or Issue

Many stories are about problems or issues that need to be resolved. Finding the story line includes asking questions that are slightly different from the questions asked for goal-oriented stories.

After you've read the material, ask, "What is the problem that needs to be resolved?" (the end occurs when the problem is resolved). "What do the characters do to resolve the problem?" (the middle of the story). "When did the problem become apparent?" (the beginning of the story).

In *The Color Purple*, Celie is in an abusive relationship with Mr. That's the problem. Toward the end of the film and book, Celie resolves this problem by leaving. That's a resolution to this problem. By looking at just this much of the story line, you can see a clear beginning (Celie enters into this relationship) and a clear ending (she leaves).

Part of this problem is connected to Celie's low self-esteem, and Mr.'s sending away her dear sister, Nettie, who was Celie's only friend, the only person who really loved her. When Celie thinks that Nettie hasn't written to her (since Mr. is hiding all the letters), she has no one to help her. The introduction of Nettie, and of Celie's lack of self-esteem, and Nettie's going away are all part of the material we need to know before we can see the development of the story. So all this information is still part of the beginning of the story, which defines the problem.

So what happens in the middle? To find the middle, ask, "How does the character get from the problem in the beginning to the resolution of the problem at the end?" What does the character do? What happens to the character? Who influences the character? What developments occur to change the character from "the character with a problem" to "the character who has resolved the problem"?

Again, in the case of *The Color Purple*, much of the development occurs because of the introduction of Shug, who likes Celie, who helps raise her self-esteem, and who helps her find the letters from Nettie. This relationship makes up much of the middle of the film. When Celie finds the letters, and then discovers the courage to stand up to Mr., we are seeing a process that will lead to the resolution of the problem and the reunion with Nettie—which happens at the end.

Some films with problem-oriented or issue-oriented story

lines include *A Room with a View* (Lucy needs to find her own identity in order to recognize that George is the right man for her, not Cecil); *The Elephant Man* (John Merrick needs to find acceptance and recognition of his humanity); *One Flew Over the Cuckoo's Nest* (the patients need to escape from the tyranny of Nurse Ratched).

When you work with these story lines, use words such as "the need," "the problem," "the issue," and ask, "What has to be learned or changed?" In most of these stories there's a very strong main character whose need or recognition of a problem actually creates the story. McMurphy, in *One Flew Over the Cuckoo's Nest*, makes decisions and actions that allow the story to happen. If he weren't there, the patients would continue playing cards, going to therapy meetings, and taking their medication—thus, no story.

Some story lines are even more subtle.

Look for a Journey

Some story lines place most of their emphasis on the transformational journey of a character. The story comes from the journey rather than from defining a clear-cut goal. But even journeys have beginnings, middles, and ends.

Another set of questions can help you discover these story lines. In this case, you may want first to find the middle of the story, asking, "What happens to my character in this story? How is my character changed? influenced? transformed? Who helps in this transformation? Is there anyone who hinders it?" Most of these answers will lead you to the middle of your story. The middle will develop all of these transforming relationships, and show how (and usually why) the transformation is occurring.

Now ask questions that will help you find the beginning of the story. "When did my character begin on this journey? What was the motivation? Did something happen that forced the character to begin this change?"

Then ask questions about the end. "When do I know that the character has changed? What clues clarify that this character has been transformed? Is there a particular moment or scene in the story that shows an end to this particular journey?"

Journey stories can be the most difficult to adapt because they're more subtle. They can easily lose their story lines. They become development episodes that don't add up to a cohesive story line ("one action"). Sometimes there isn't a clear climax, so you might enjoy the journey, but when you get there, you wonder whether, and where, you've actually arrived.

At the same time, if we like the characters, journey stories can be very satisfying because we clearly see how characters develop and how transformations occur. Think about the award-winning journey stories of *GoodFellas, Driving Miss Daisy*, and *Dances With Wolves*. If you liked the characters, you probably liked the film.

Many story lines combine aspects of the goal-oriented, problem-oriented, and journey stories. Chances are, one or all of the questions mentioned above will help you find your story line. You can also use these questions to help you identify adaptations that didn't work. Were their story lines cohesive and well defined (even though they may have been subtle?) Where did they swerve from their story line?

CREATE THREE ACTS

As you define the beginnings, middles, and ends, you are also defining Act One, Act Two, and Act Three of your story. You are beginning to put your story line into dramatic form.

By defining your story line in these dramatic terms, you are beginning to craft and shape the story into a screenplay. In its simplest terms, Act One refers to the material that sets up your story. It introduces your characters. It establishes the problem, issue, need, or goal. It gives you the information you need to know before you start developing the story.

Act Two develops the story. It develops relationships. It shows the actions that the character is willing to do to resolve the problem or reach the goal. It sets up the obstacles that create problems for the character.

Act Three pays off the story, it resolves it. Hopefully there's a dramatic build leading to a climax or a "big finish" that makes the ending exciting, intense, and/or emotionally satisfying. This act intensifies the conflict. Raises the stakes. Leads to an inevitable conclusion.

Most of the screenplay will focus on the development of the story, so Act Two will be longer than the other acts (in a two-hour film, Act Two will usually be about sixty pages long, or one hour if you figure about one minute of screen time to a page). Since Act Three is usually the most exciting, the fastest-paced, and most intense, it will generally be the shortest act. In a two-hour film, it's usually between twenty and thirty minutes long. And Act One usually runs twenty-five to thirty-five minutes.

Dividing up the story in this way, let's look at the three-act structure in *Dances With Wolves*.

ACT ONE: *Sets Up the Situation*—Lieutenant Dunbar wants to see the frontier and is sent there. He begins the journey that will change his life.

ACT TWO: *Develops the Situation and Relationships*—Lieutenant Dunbar develops relationships with the Indians. He's transformed by their way of life.

ACT THREE: *Shows Consequences of Decisions Made in Act Two*—The lieutenant returns to his post, where he is captured by white men who accuse him of treason and of "turning Injun." He's beaten and chained but finally rescued by the Indians. He decides to leave the Indians, since his presence is a liability to them.

LOOK FOR THE CLIMAX

Once you begin to find the shape of the material and have a sense of where it will fit into your story, begin looking for key events in the story that are dramatic, active, exciting, and cinematic.

These events will begin to form the backbone of your story, or what is often referred to as the "story spine." I find it most helpful first to identify the scene (or scenes) at the end of the story that clarify that a character has reached the goal, resolved the problem, or ended the particular journey. This is the climax of the story.

The climax is particularly important in film, since a rising dramatic line that ends with a "big finish" gives a sense of "rush" and excitement and culmination to all the development that has gone before. If you have a strong climactic scene in your book or play, use it.

Generally, action films will contain the strongest dramatic climax. To understand why they work, think about how you felt while watching the ending of such films as *High Noon*, the *Die Hard* films, or any of the James Bond films.

Not every story will lend itself to this kind of a big finish. But no matter what sort of story you use, be careful not to let the action slow down or dissipate at the end. The idea is to create a climax that builds in action and intensity.

You won't always find the climax at the end of the story. Sometimes a novelist ends the story, and then writes some more about character and theme before the book ends. Some of the screenwriter's search for the ending might include looking for big scenes or moments within the story that can be shaped into a climax. Sometimes a screenwriter must work backward from the end of the book, searching for the scene that resolves the problem or ends the journey.

IDENTIFY THE CATALYST

What scenes establish the problem? How does the problem get set up in the original material? The scene where this occurs—the "catalyst"—is the scene that starts your story, or the first event that begins the story spine. In detective and action-adventure stories it is usually a crime or some other illegal activity that occurs. The main character then enters to resolve the problem. In *Out of Africa*, the scene where Karen Blixen goes to Africa is the catalyst, as is the one where Lieutenant Dunbar heads for the frontier, where Jessica falls into the well, where Lucy meets George in *A Room with a View*, and where the men in *Deliverance* head out for the wilderness.

Generally the catalyst will be placed within the first ten or fifteen pages of the screenplay. Until it occurs we won't know what the story is about.

IDENTIFY TRANSITION SCENES

What scenes move the story from Act One to Act Two, and from Act Two to Act Three? These are called transition scenes. Since each Act focuses on different material, these scenes help change the focus from one act to another. In *Dances With Wolves*, Lieutenant Dunbar decides to get dressed in his military uniform and go out to meet the Indians. This scene moves him from the action of the first act where he watches the Indians in the distance to his decision to meet them.

This scene is the First Turning Point and it begins Act Two. It turns the action around and establishes a different focus for the next act. Notice that it's an active scene. Lieutenant Dunbar makes a decision and takes an action. The action in Act Two will develop around his relationship with the Indians.

What scenes show the character confronting the consequences of actions taken in Act Two? In *Dances With Wolves*, Lieutenant Dunbar returns to his post in order to get his journal, and is immediately captured by the white soldiers. His decisions in Act Two have led to this confrontation. This scene is the Second Turning Point. His Act Two transformation has brought him into conflict with white soldiers. The scene where he returns sets the action of Act Three, which includes beatings, interrogations, greater jeopardy, and finally an escape.

Notice that each of these turning-point scenes shows a decision made by the main character: Lieutenant Dunbar goes out to meet the Indians; Lieutenant Dunbar decides to return to his post to get his journal. Decision scenes create strong turning points. If you find them, you'll probably want to use them.

You might think of these transition scenes as "hinge scenes." The story hinges on these important scenes, which move us from one place to another. Such scenes won't always exist in the original material; you may need to create them. But they're important because they help shape and focus the material, and help you keep the story moving through the setup, development, and payoff.

In a two-hour film your First Turning Point will generally occur about thirty minutes into the film, and your Second Turning Point will usually occur about twenty to thirty minutes from the end of the film. From my observations, if a first act is too long (say forty minutes or more in a two-hour film), there will not be adequate time to develop the middle, and audiences often say that the film "lagged," or "slowed down."

You can test this concept by looking at the film *Awakenings*. The First Turning Point occurs about forty-six minutes into the film, when Leonard takes the medicine and awakens. It's quite a late turning point, although there are interesting scenes and considerable information in the beginning. When I taught this film at a Writers Guild seminar, a high proportion of those attending thought the beginning was "slow" and felt that the long first act condensed the important second act about Leonard's development and transformation. In cases such as this, the balance seems just a bit off. And this "little bit off" can give audiences a sense of uneasiness, or disappointment. (I should add that I loved this film, but would have liked a tightened Act One and an expanded Act Two.)

If an Act Three is less than fifteen minutes long, there's usually not enough time to create a strong build to the climax. If it's more than thirty minutes long, the tension can begin to dissipate. To see how this can happen, you might want to look at how the tension dissipates toward the end of *The Color Purple* and the end of *Kiss of the Spider Woman*, from the novel by Manuel Puig.

SEPARATE THE STORY LINES

In a novel or play, there is often more than one story line. There are relationship stories. There are action stories. There are stories that carry an idea. We might say that most novels will have stories that advance the action or move the story forward, and stories that dimensionalize characters and convey theme.

As I mentioned before, a strong film will balance the elements of direction and dimensionality. The story line that gives movement can be called the plot line, or A story. The story line(s) that give dimensionality to the story by developing characters and relationships and theme are the subplots.

Generally there will be several subplots, perhaps B, C, and D story lines. Be careful if you have more than four subplots, since too many subplots can make a film muddy, confused, or difficult to follow.

When you are pulling out the story lines from your source material, look first for the A story line, one that gives movement and direction. Then begin finding the structure for the subplot lines.

EXPLICITLY DRAMATIC STORY LINES

In order to discuss story concepts, I want to look at three books that have strong dramatic story lines. These are by no means great novels, but they did create highly commercial films because of story lines that adapted easily to the screen. By using these novels as models for an easy adaptation, we can also begin to see ways to strengthen the story lines of more difficult adaptations. The three are *Three Days of the Condor*, from a book by James Grady, *The Towering Inferno* (based on two books, *The Tower*, by Richard Martin Stern, and *The Glass Inferno*, by Thomas N. Scortia and Frank M. Robinson), and *Die Hard 2* (based on *58 Minutes* by Walter Wager). What do these three have in common that makes them highly adaptable?

1. Each of them takes place over a very short period of time, from an evening to three days. (*58 Minutes* actually covers more than fifty-eight minutes—it covers an evening.) The shorter the period of time in a novel, the easier it is to keep a tight focus to the story.

2. Each of these stories has a rising dramatic line. The suspense quickens, the tension builds, the story gets more and more exciting as it goes along.

3. Each of these stories has a clear three-act structure that supports this buildup. A clear problem is set up within the first fifteen minutes of the film (the murder of the CIA team in *Three Days of the Condor*, the fire on the top floor in *The Towering Inferno*, and the terrorist attack in *58 Minutes*). The protagonists try to resolve the problem throughout the second act as the stakes get higher. And the third act is a fast-paced payoff, culminating in a strong climax and a short resolution.

4. The stakes in these stories are clear. There is nothing ambiguous about what will happen if the protagonist doesn't resolve the problem—hundreds, perhaps thousands, will die, justice won't be done, our hero will be killed, there will be massive destruction of life and property. Chaos will reign.

5. The main character's action is integrally connected with the story line. The protagonist causes the story line to be resolved. There is no passive hero here, but an active fighting hero

who changes the direction of the story and makes the climax happen.

Almost all of the action of the hero advances the story. The main character has a strong intention. We know what he wants, and we root for his character from the very beginning. Again, there are no ambiguities.

This is not to say that you can only adapt heroic action-adventure stories. But it is important to understand what makes an easy adaptation and why, in order to tackle more complex story problems. Films need movement, and movement comes from the story line. If there is no story, character and theme by themselves cannot carry the movie.

Let's look at *Die Hard 2* in more detail. In this film, both the A story and the subplots (particularly the B story line about hero McClane's wife) are clear.

ACT ONE—The terrorists arrive. They begin their preparations.

FIRST TURNING POINT—They destroy the control tower, leading to . . .

ACT TWO—The stakes get higher. McClane runs into conflict with the authorities at the airport. Development focuses on trying to save the planes and trying to stop the terrorists by finding their headquarters and capturing them.

SECOND TURNING POINT—Shows McClane discovering terrorists' headquarters as they prepare to get away in a 747. This discovery leads to . . .

ACT THREE—McClane chases the terrorists, confronts them, and fights with them as their plane starts to leave; he finally blows up the plane, thus destroying the villains in a grand climax.

This A story line is reinforced by a B story line about McClane's wife, who is on one of the airplanes that is running out of fuel.

This B story also has a three-act structure:

ACT ONE—Establishes the wife on the plane.

ACT TWO—Shows that fuel is running out, the plane can't land, and the weather is getting worse.

ACT THREE—Shows the plane almost out of fuel.

CLIMAX—The plane lands and McClane is reunited with his wife.

Not all the events in the film are exactly the same as in the book. Characters are changed (in the book, the main character, named Malone, is divorced), the setting is different (the book takes place at a New York airport, the film in Washington, D.C.), and even the subplot is different, since in the book, it is McClane's daughter on the plane, not his wife.

For the film, the subplot was expanded by showing more of the wife and by creating a relationship between the wife and a reporter whom she disliked. This B story is very workable, since it personalizes the story, provides tension, and contains a clear beginning, middle, and end.

Sometimes the story you're adapting doesn't have the beginning, middle, and end in chronological order.

In the short story "The Greatest Gift," the basis for *It's a Wonderful Life*, the entire story takes place on the night when George contemplates suicide and an angel gives him the opportunity to reflect on the importance of his life. In this case, events had to be reordered to create a beginning, middle, and end and to expand the story into a two-hour film. This meant looking for clues about events that had taken place in the past. Since George was married, it implied a subplot about meeting, courting, and marrying his wife. Since the story mentioned his business, this could imply a subplot about coming into the business, having problems with it, and resolving the problems.

What if your story doesn't have a clear beginning, middle, or end? What if it has a third act that slows down and fades out rather than building to a dramatic climax? What if much of the story contains episodes that don't add up to a cohesive story line?

Don't despair—yet. If it's difficult to find the overall shape, begin looking for the smaller shapes that are in the story. Instead of starting with the big picture (the beginnings, middles, and ends, the three-act structure), begin with the smaller picture. Begin with the story arcs.

FINDING THE STORY ARC

Sometimes a story arc or the dramatic arc is the same as a story spine. In the beginning of C. S. Forester's *The African Queen*, Rose tells Alnut that she wants to blow up the boat *The Louisa*. At the end of the book, they do. This connection between the beginning and the end of a story line is a story arc. If I were to sketch this dramatic arc, it would look like this:

Rose wants to blow   At the end, she does
up *The Louisa*

All the events within this story arc are connected to the objective (to blow up the boat). All the events bring us closer to the climax.

In *A Room with a View*, there's an overall story arc that is also the same as the story spine. This spine or arc is established by asking a question toward the beginning of the film, ("Will Lucy marry George?") and answering the question at the end ("Yes").

Notice that the story arc focuses on a particular story and connects the beginning with the end. The strongest dramatic stories will combine the story arcs and the story spine so that they are interchangeable.

But there are variations on this idea. Within the story spine (or overall story arc) will be a number of smaller story arcs.

The buffalo hunt in *Dances With Wolves* would be considered a smaller story arc. It takes up about fifteen to twenty minutes of screen time. All the events from the time that Lieutenant Dunbar hears the buffalo until he eats the heart and retells the story of killing it are part of that particular story arc.

This story arc about "hunting the buffalo" is part of a larger story arc about "developing relationships with the Indians" (the Act Two story arc) and it's also part of the story arc that is the same as the story spine—about Lieutenant Dunbar on his journey of discovery of the outer and inner frontier.

When you can't find the largest story arc, begin looking for the smaller ones. A story arc has movement and direction, and can begin to form a story line. *Gone With the Wind* has a series of smaller arcs and a rather subtle overall arc to its story. If you were the original adaptor of *Gone With the Wind*, you might begin by looking at the series of arcs within the book. For instance, it, like the film, is divided almost in half. The first focuses on the war, the second half on Reconstruction.

One might say that by the end of the book, an old era of the South was gone, but a new era that was to define the South for the next hundred years was beginning. This gives an overall arc to the book. Within this arc are three smaller arcs that could be sketched this way:

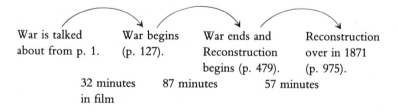

War is talked about from p. 1.	War begins (p. 127).	War ends and Reconstruction begins (p. 479).	Reconstruction over in 1871 (p. 975).
	32 minutes in film	87 minutes	57 minutes

But the book itself is 1,024 pages long. What happens in the last fifty pages? Bonnie dies, Melanie gets pregnant again, Melanie dies, Scarlett (finally) realizes it's Rhett she loves, Rhett leaves her.

These are all relational stories that end the book, and that also have their own story arcs. Sometimes these are called "character arcs," but technically a "character arc" has more to do with character transformations than character actions. Here we want to focus specifically on story arcs that refer to events that create a story line.

In *Gone With the Wind* there are a number of different subplot story arcs that revolve around specific characters. The Ashley-Scarlett story arc begins almost immediately in the book, on page 5, when Scarlett expresses her interest in Ashley, and it continues until page 1,016, when she says, "I never loved Ashley."

The Rhett relationship line begins on page 98, when they meet, and ends on page 1,023, when he says, "My dear, I don't give a damn."

The Melanie relationship line begins on page 5, when Scarlett is told that Ashley will marry Melanie, and it ends on page 1,001, when Melanie dies.

Think about the film for a moment. What is your overall impression of the film when you reflect on Part One and Part Two? Personally, I find the first half of the film more dynamic, with clearer direction, and a stronger context. Why? Certainly this sketching of the dramatic arcs has shown that they move well throughout the story. Why, then, would Part One be stronger than Part Two? It is because some of these arcs have stronger *intentionality* from the characters. This intentionality gives more direction to the story, and creates stronger story arcs.

INTENTIONALITY

Intentionality can best be defined by asking the question "What does the character want?" Characters with strong desires usually take strong actions to achieve them. They go after their intention, or goal. When a character declares what she or he wants, that declaration begins a story arc that won't be completed until the intention is realized.

This intention can create a story arc that is the same as the story spine (as we mentioned with goal-oriented story lines), or it can create smaller story arcs. In *Driving Miss Daisy*, Hoke wants to drive Miss Daisy. He gets the job, and she finally allows him to drive her. This story arc, established by his intention, takes up about ten to fifteen minutes of screen time.

In order to understand intention in relationship to the dramatic arc, it's first necessary to separate plot line (or story) arcs from subplot (or relationship) arcs.

For the first half of *Gone With the Wind*, the story arc is for the South to win the war. From the time when the war breaks out until it ends we are carried through the story by this intention, which is reinforced by Scarlett's love of Tara. The destruction of the South implies the destruction of Tara and all it stands for.

When Scarlett returns to Tara after the burning of Atlanta, she vows to save it—and puts considerable effort into doing so. She searches for food, learns to milk a cow, kills a Yankee soldier, offers herself to Rhett (who has said he's not a marrying man), and even marries her sister's rich beau—all to satisfy her intention to save Tara. The intention of the South, and the intention of Scarlett, is quite clear for the first half of the book, and about two-thirds of the film.

What happens after the war is over? The overall arc of the story becomes less clear, less dynamic. In the book, there is clearer intentionality for the last half of the story because there are stronger story lines about Rhett and Scarlett's courting of the Yankees to regain some of what they'd lost. There's a strong story arc about the creation of the Ku Klux Klan (Ashley and Scarlett's husband, Frank Kennedy, and most of the other Southern men are part of the founding of the Klan). And there's a story arc that shows the men's intention to get the Yankee Republicans out of power and have more say in the new Southern government. All of these smaller arcs in the book add up to a larger overall arc of the Southerners' desire to regain some sort of dignity and power over their lives, to regain at least something of what was "gone with the wind."

In the film, however, the relationship arcs are the focus of the last third of the film. And relationship arcs rarely create as much movement as story arcs. As you watch the last third of the film, look for places where the story arc is working well, and others where it seems to dissipate and lose direction. For instance, there's a rather clear, nicely worked out arc when Scarlett is attacked at the shantytown. As a result, that night the men (Ashley, Frank, and others) go to clean out the place, Rhett discovers that the Yankees have a plot to catch them, he warns them, Frank is killed, Ashley is shot, Belle Watling, the madam, helps give the men their alibi, and in the last scene of this arc, Melanie personally thanks her.

Notice how every scene advances the action. Compare this strong story arc with scenes that have less movement and intentionality, such as scenes of Rhett showing off Bonnie, taking Bonnie to Europe, or teaching Bonnie to ride. Although these scenes reveal character, from a story viewpoint they are more episodic and don't have the same forward direction.

Keep the story arcs going until the end of the film, even though some of them may be small. Anytime an audience is within a story arc, they'll be paying attention because every action is related.

You might want to look at the end of *Dances With Wolves* to see how one additional story arc at the end of the film kept it from lagging. The beginning of Act Three shows Lieutenant Dunbar's capture. This forms an exciting story arc that continues until he's rescued by the Indians. Now, notice, we're near the end of the film, but the story arc has ended. How is the writer going to continue to keep us attentive? He waits a few minutes while Dunbar comes home, reflects on his experience, and thinks about what he's going to do about it. Then one more story arc is begun, which might be called "Getting Ready to Leave." There are only about three minutes between returning home and getting ready to leave, but just when the audience could have lost interest, a new story arc is begun. This story arc then shows preparations, saying good-bye, the exchange of gifts, and Dunbar and Stands With A Fist riding away. This story arc has additional excitement because it's intercut with a story arc about the soldiers looking for the Indians' winter camp.

Dances With Wolves felt shorter than its three-hour length partly because of a strong structure and a good use of story arcs.

LOOK FOR SCENE SEQUENCES

Once you know the structure of the plots and subplots, and have identified the story arcs, begin looking for *scene sequences* within the story. A scene sequence can be defined as a series of scenes on the same idea with a clear beginning, middle, and end. The shantytown scenes in *Gone With the Wind* create a scene sequence. So do the scenes about the escape during the burning of Atlanta, and the "Melanie has her baby" sequence. Scene sequences give the maximum momentum to a story. Momentum means that each scene implies the next one—one leads to another. Each scene advances the action. Each scene goes somewhere.

For example, when you construct your screenplay, you'll usually have some A story scenes (plot line) interrupted by subplot scenes from the B, C, and D story lines. In *Gone With the Wind* you'll see some scenes about the war (A story scenes), followed by a scene about Scarlett and Rhett (a B story scene), followed perhaps by a scene about Scarlett and Ashley (a C story scene). If you were to label the order of scenes in your script, the interrelationship of scenes might look like this:

A C C B A C B A A C B A B

In *Gone With the Wind* you notice almost immediately that there's an A story scene that mentions the war, another A story scene shows further discussion of the war at the party, a third shows the call to enlist, a fourth scene shows the men leaving, and a fifth shows the women receiving the news that one of the men has died. Notice that all of these scenes are connected. Each scene logically leads to the next.

But ordinarily these scenes are scattered throughout the film. It may take thirty-five minutes of screen time to play these scenes because they are interrupted by the B story scenes about Rhett: Scarlett meets Rhett at the party, he overhears her confession to Ashley, he meets her again later, he reenters her life during the war.

And they're interrupted by C story scenes about Ashley: Scarlett hears he's getting married, she decides to confess her love to him, she does so and he refuses her, he marries Melanie.

Most scenes in films are played this way, moving back and forth between the plot and subplot scenes. This is a simplified analysis, since some scenes have material from the A, B, and C stories in one scene, others have scenes that are only A story or B story scenes. But for the purposes of our analysis, you might find it helpful to imagine each of these as separate scenes.

You gain momentum from the story line because each A story scene implies the next A story scene, each B story scene implies the next B story scene, and so on.

A scene sequence plays all the scenes from one story line in a row, without interruption from other subplot scenes. You can have a scene sequence of A story scenes, or of subplot scenes.

The scene sequence will have a beginning, a middle, an end, a rising dramatic line, and a certain amount of tension implied within this dramatic line. Scene sequences in *Gone With the Wind* include "Melanie has her baby," "The burning of Atlanta," "Rhett saves Ashley from the Yankees." These scenes are not interrupted by subplot scenes, but focus on one main action.

A scene sequence needs to be long enough to create a rising dramatic line, but short enough to sustain interest. Generally, scene sequences are usually about three to seven pages of script. Most psychological thrillers and action-adventures will have several scene sequences, since they give the most movement and drive to a story. But you can find them in any genre, including comedy, sci-fi, fantasy, or horror.

You will probably want to use any scene sequences you find within a story, since they're intrinsically dramatic. Look for any group of scenes that has a smaller story arc with a beginning, middle, and end.

In *Stand by Me*, the boys begin walking across a bridge and are almost hit by a train. This creates a wonderful scene sequence that, on film, plays for about three and a half to four minutes.

In the book, it reads like this. I'm writing it out in this way in order to show the implicit three-act structure within the story. I'm also cutting a sentence here and there for the sake of brevity.

ACT ONE—Establishes the situation. "The rail was mute. . . . We went out onto the trestle single file. . . . I started to feel dizzy and disoriented. . . . I squatted and made a fist around the rail on my left."

FIRST TURNING POINT—"It thrummed in my hand. It was thrumming so hard that it was like gripping a bundle of deadly metallic snakes. . . ."

ACT TWO—Develops the fear, shows the boys running, trying to escape the oncoming train. "I've been scared since, badly scared, but I've never been as scared as I was in that moment, holding that hot live rail. . . . I shot to my feet. I screamed, 'TRAIN.' . . . Now it was right behind Vern. We were past the halfway point and for the first time I heard the train. . . . 'Awwww, shit!' Vern screamed. 'Run, you pussy!' I yelled. . . . 'I can't. I'll fall.' 'Run faster. . . .' "

SECOND TURNING POINT—"The train was very loud now."

ACT THREE—Builds the excitement and the stakes. "The freight's electric horn suddenly spanked the air . . . with one long loud blast. . . . And then Chris was below us and to the right, and they were both mouthing a single word and the word was 'Jump!' . . . The trestle began to shake as the train charged across it."

CLIMAX—"We jumped."

RESOLUTION—"When it was gone—when I was sure it was gone—I raised my head like a soldier coming out of his foxhole at the end of a day-long artillery barrage. Vern was still plastered into the dirt, shivering. Chris was sitting cross-legged between us, one hand on Vern's sweaty neck, the other still on mine. When Vern finally sat up, shaking all over and licking his lips compulsively, Chris said, 'What you guys think we drink those Cokes? Could anybody use one besides me?' We all thought we could use one."

When you read this sequence you may think that it is frightening, exciting, perhaps even makes your heart beat faster. If you have this response to something in a story, you will probably want to include it in the film.

You can also find implied scene sequences that can be built up and expanded for the script. For instance, there are several descriptions in *Out of Africa* that could be played out to create a scene sequence if desired.

"The grasshoppers came again; for two or three months we had continued attacks of them on the farm." You could create an exciting short or long sequence of the "attack by the grasshoppers," particularly if you wanted to focus more on the problems of the plantation. Here you would probably condense the time of two or three months to one grasshopper attack. The beginning of the scene sequence could include the news or sighting of the grasshoppers, the middle could be the attack, and the end could be the final battle with them or the action taken to overcome their destruction. You would probably need six to seven pages of script to play this out.

Here's another description, one that was made into a scene sequence in the film: "To Denys Finch-Hatton, I owe what was, I think, the greatest, the most transporting pleasure of my life on the farm: I flew with him over Africa." This was turned into the airplane flight sequence, one of my favorite scenes from the film. The airplane sequence does not have the strong structure of the *Stand by Me* sequence, although it does have a clear beginning and end and a rising sense of wonder.

You can create scene sequences out of courtship scenes, battle scenes, chase scenes, or any kind of scenes that contain dramatic development that builds to a climactic moment.

BUILDING UP THE CLIMAX

Earlier I discussed finding the climax of the story. If it's a dramatic climax, use it. But you may need to change a climax in a story to make it work.

The climax in a novel or play does not need to have the same dramatic buildup as in a film. Sometimes the adaptor has to reorder events or add to the actions in a book in order to create a dramatic build. In *Stand by Me*, events were slightly reordered, so the climax of the confrontation between Gordy and the older boys was toward the end of the sequence. Compare the differences between the sequence of events of the book and the film as illustrated in the chart on page 101.

Notice that Gordy, the main character, is carrying most of the action in the film that was originally given to Chris in the story. In the film Gordy cries, not Chris, Gordy fires the gun, not Chris. Notice also that the scene in the film builds to the confrontation between Gordy and the boys by placing the crying and discussion before the climax, rather than after.

The film ends with a resolution phrase that sums up much of the experience: "I never had any friends later on like the ones I had when I was twelve. Jesus, did you?" This phrase is actually in the middle of the story.

You want your climax to come at the end of the screenplay. That sometimes means reordering events. After the climax occurs, it's time to end the film, to wrap up loose ends, to go home. A resolution needs to be short, preferably not longer than five minutes and not more than two or perhaps three scenes.

Look at the endings of the films *A Passage to India* and *The Color Purple*. Both had very long resolutions that dissipated the action. As a creative exercise, see what you could cut from

BOOK	FILM
Lightning	Some rain
Vern sees body	Vern sees body
Rain	Gordy cries
Ace comes	Gordy discusses Dad, death
Gordy says, "Suck my fat one"	Ace and Billy come
Ace threatens the four boys	Ace pulls knife on Chris
Chris fires pistol	Gordy shoots gun
Chris fires as they get closer	Gordy says, "Suck my fat one"
Hail	They leave body
Vern and Teddy run	Adult narrator talks and writes about Chris
Chris and Gordy stay	
Chris cries	He plays with sons
They argue about taking body	
They leave for home	
Gordy talks to father	
Big boys beat up on kids	
Adult narrator tells that Chris, Teddy, Vern, all are dead	

these resolutions to tighten them. In *The Color Purple* I would define the climax as the point when Celie leaves Mr. All that really needs to occur in the resolution is to get Nettie back home. I think it could be done in a much shorter resolution—but this would take some drastic rethinking.

LOOK FOR THE IMPLIED SCENE

Sometimes a book contains so many scenes that all you need to do is pick and choose the ones to carry the story cinematically.

At other times, scenes need to be created. You can always make them up, just as you would in an original screenplay. But books and plays are always implying scenes that are not shown. Since these scenes are naturally part of a story, they are clues you can use in your writing.

Sometimes scenes are implied when a character briefly mentions a friend, or some incident from childhood, or simply says she or he had a bad day at work. All of these mentions can be made into scenes.

Scarlett gets married three times, which means three weddings of one sort or another. She mentions one of them (it is shown in the film), but not the other two. But they did happen. A writer might decide to show them.

In the play *The Little Foxes*, Zan is told to go to Baltimore to bring her father home from the hospital. In the film, this scene is played out.

In *Out of Africa*, there's a line that implies a dramatic scene: "My old cook, Esa, was murdered." If the plantation subplot had been expanded in this story line, this scene could have been played out for additional conflict.

In *A Room with a View*, Miss Bartlett confronts George about his insult (the kiss) to her cousin, Lucy. "At the critical moment Miss Bartlett opened her own door, and her voice said: 'I wish one word with you in the drawing-room, Mr. Emerson, please.'

"Soon their footsteps returned, and Miss Bartlett said: 'Goodnight, Mr. Emerson.' "

If the point of view had been expanded to accommodate scenes about George or Miss Bartlett (without Lucy in the scene), the scene these lines imply could have been shown.

INTEGRATING PLOT AND SUBPLOT

In *My Left Foot,* we see a story about a man with cerebral palsy struggling for identity and love. That is the major focus of both the book and the movie. Christy Brown had another important story in his life—the story of meeting Mary, falling in love, and getting married. Unfortunately for dramatic purposes, the subplot happened after Christy had achieved a certain measure of success and had resolved some of his earlier struggles.

Ordinarily the threading together of plot and subplot would be happening throughout the story line. But occasionally a true-life story will have two important plot lines that did not happen at the same time in the subject's life.

The writers of the film *My Left Foot,* Shane Connaughton and Jim Sheridan, must have recognized this problem. In order to resolve it, they began the film in the present, establishing Christy and Mary, and then played his struggles in flashback. Throughout the film we continue to go back to short scenes between Christy and Mary as their relationship develops, finally leading up to him asking her to cancel her plans in order to go out with him. In the last scene they're together, joyous, drinking champagne, and an epilogue at the end tells us that they did get married.

Although I personally believe that flashbacks are often misused and overused, they can provide a solution to many of these particular true-life story problems. Sometimes flashbacks can be used as a frame to start and end the movie.

Sometimes, too, flashbacks can be used all the way through, actually structuring two plot lines, where one plays itself out in the flashbacks and another plays itself out in present time. In *The Woman He Loved,* about the Duke and Duchess of Windsor, the duchess tells the story of her relationship with the Duke of

Windsor in present time while flashbacks show the story. In *Lucy and Desi: Before the Laughter*, a similar problem was encountered. How do you tell the story of Desi and Lucy? The success of the television series was clearly a high point of their lives and would need to be dealt with, but the series came after a great many struggles and a long journey toward success that took place over many years.

Flashback solved this problem: in the present tense Lucy and Desi prepared for the filming of their first show, a story with its own structure and development. Flashbacks were used to go back to key events in their lives, which also had their own structure. The present-tense scenes helped structure and frame the flashback scenes, which were somewhat episodic. Without some kind of frame or structuring, they would have seemed like random scenes from two lives, instead of forming a cohesive narrative line.

CHANGING PLOT TO SUBPLOT

Many novels and even plays are about relationships or about the characters' inner psychological state. The story is not as important as the understanding of the characters. Many of these works will still contain some story thread that weaves throughout the work, but it might be small and seemingly inconsequential.

When adapting such material, this thread is where you begin your work on the story. Although, as I've said earlier, generally the A story is the story line that gives movement and direction to a film and the subplots give dimensionality, occasionally a small subplot in a book can become the important A story that makes the film work.

If you aren't getting enough movement from the focus of the novel or play, see if there's some small subplot that can be built up, perhaps even making it your plot line for the film. This will work best if the subplot revolves around, or can be changed to revolve around, your main character.

In *Stand by Me*, the movement of the film comes from the story line about searching for a dead body. In terms of the meaning, this is the least important part of both the novella and the film. But from a story viewpoint, the structuring of this story thread made the film work. We never lost sight of this story line. It had a strong three-act structure, beginning about five minutes into the film and ending about five minutes before the film ended. Although it didn't take a great deal of screen time, I would still analyze this as the A story of the film, because it provided movement and direction.

Most of the film, and the book, dealt with more thematic issues. There's a subplot about Gordy as a burgeoning writer. Another subplot concerns the boys' relationships with their fathers. These subplots were probably the reason why the film touched us and involved us. And they were the core of the book and the film. But without the story thread, the film wouldn't have worked.

This A story line does not need to take up the most screen time, but it does need to be present throughout the script. It needs to be well structured, and it needs to give the required movement to the story. If the story seems to lag or seems slow-moving, chances are that the story thread isn't yet in balance.

Some films where the story thread did not seem strong enough were *Out of Africa*, *Hope and Glory*, and *Avalon*. Although I think the films are in many ways brilliant, there seemed to be problems with their movement and balance. The reviews mentioned these problems, and when I teach the films, I receive the same responses from people in my classes.

I have often thought that the subplot about the plantation needed to be stronger in *Out of Africa*. Certainly it was an important part of the book. It had the potential to give structure, shape, and movement to the film, particularly since the plantation fire is a strong climax to this plot line. It would not have meant eliminating the rich relationship stories within the film, but it would have meant some rethinking of the relationship of plot and subplot.

Sometimes a film gets almost all of its movement from the

subplot lines, even though the subplot doesn't revolve around the main characters. If you look at *Hope and Glory*, you'll notice that most of the movement is coming from the relationship subplot about Dawn and Bruce—their meeting, courtship, her pregnancy, and their marriage. In *Avalon* there's movement from the business-relationship subplot of Izzy and Jules. But these are not the main characters, and the relationship plot line ended twenty minutes before the end of the film.

You may want to watch these three films again in order to check your reaction to them. When did they seem to lag, if they did for you? When were you most attentive to them? When were you least attentive?

The relationship scenes in all these films are very captivating, and they will probably hold you for most of the extended scenes. Be aware of when you stop being carried through the film. From my experience of other thematic films, I have found that strengthening and balancing the story line is one of the best ways to keep these lags from occurring.

The key word throughout this discussion is *balance*. How much movement do you need to involve the audience and carry them throughout the film? How much thematic weight do you need in the film in order to say what you have to say? Where is the balance between story movement and theme and character focus? If the story lags or is unclear, the balance has not yet been found.

RAISING THE STAKES

Many novels and some plays are "soft"—they lack a strong dramatic story line or big stakes. You can get more drama out of a story by raising the stakes.

In many adaptations, such as *High Noon*, *The Most Dangerous Game*, and *Rear Window*, the stakes are raised by adding a love interest. But there are other ways to raise the stakes.

In *It's a Wonderful Life* the dramatic subplot was intensified by raising the stakes for George. In the short story, George was "sick of everything. I'm stuck here in this mudhole for life, doing the same dull work day after day." The film raised these stakes by showing George's desire to see the world. In the short story, George is a clerk at the bank. In the film, he owns the bank. And it raised the stakes by putting George's reputation on the line, as well as the success of the bank. The film made the brother more important by making him a war hero. And the emotional pitch of the entire story was raised in the film— George is more despairing, the uncle more incompetent, Mary more concerned, the parents more despondent, the town in a more desperate situation.

KEEP THE STORY SIMPLE

Novels can handle complex stories and themes. A novel has more time to explain, to give information, to clarify, even to repeat, if necessary, so the reader can follow the story. Plays, too, can deal with more complex themes, since the ideas are expressed, to a great extent, through dialogue.

For a film, it's often necessary to simplify the story. If you have a story line that takes a great deal of explanation, or a number of characters to communicate the story, consider simplifying. I believe an audience should be able to understand much of a film by looking at the moving pictures. Certainly the dialogue will round things out, give nuances, add other thematic weight, but a story that is communicated mainly through words will not be cinematic, and usually will not be understood.

Although in 1991 the complex film *Godfather III* was nominated for the Directors Guild Award as well as for several Academy Awards, in my classes almost everyone mentioned how confusing the story was. They could not follow the Immobilare plot line. They were confused about the Pope's part in the Vatican bank scandal. They didn't understand why the archbishop seemed to switch sides, at the beginning working with Michael, later working against him. They couldn't keep all the dons straight, and they were confused about who really instituted the helicopter attack. Simplifying the story would have made this film more accessible and understandable.

PINPOINT TIME CHANGES
AND CHRONOLOGY PROBLEMS

All of the concepts mentioned in this chapter apply to true-life stories. You still look for beginnings, middles, and ends as you focus the material. You look for the story arcs. You look for sequences. You look for any subplots that you can make stronger. Such subplots might be relationships that grow and change throughout the period of a person's life being portrayed. They might include themes that could be reinforced by a story line. Perhaps a theme about the person looking for success over many years could be crafted into a story line. Perhaps there's a theme about the person gaining acceptance, or becoming famous. These themes also imply story lines.

Finding the story line within true-life stories is often even more difficult than finding it within novels or plays. The latter will usually have a thread that works its way through the material. But true-life stories often don't have a clear story thread or may have too many. It's often the psychological insights that make a writer choose the material. The relationships or significance of a theme or topicality may pique a producer's interest in the material. Or it may be the subject's place in history that makes an executive choose the material, in spite of the lack of clarity about which aspect of the story, of many possible ones, should be told.

These projects need structure because they tend to be shapeless. Many of them are of epic proportions, some covering so many years in a person's life that the films need a change of actors at some point in the material. Epics begin to fall apart when they're too episodic, or when the focus is split among a variety of themes. Most of the best-known true-life stories concentrate on one story arc. *Lawrence of Arabia* focused on his time in the desert. *Gandhi* focused on his crusade for nonviolence.

Other techniques can be useful when working with bio-graphical material. If the epic begins during childhood, be particularly careful about spending too much time on the child, who might fascinate us too much. We may not want to get involved with the adult if the child actor is taking too much of the focus. (This happened to some extent with *Cinema Paradiso*.) Generally, changing an actor at any point within the first act seems workable. If the change comes much later, it can cause problems. In *GoodFellas*, the adult actor entered fifteen minutes into the film. In *My Left Foot*, the adult Christy Brown was introduced immediately, and then became the main actor by the end of Act One.

Radical time changes can be handled in a variety of ways to give movement to a story. Some films will use a frame. Perhaps the adult character is telling the story, and the body of the film is a flashback. Although this is sometimes overused, it does have the advantage of introducing the main character as an adult, and of adding a reflective tone to the film. It can give structure by framing the film as a whole, or even by bringing in the character to interject and remind us of his or her presence throughout the film. This frame can be structured both to enclose sections of a script and to give movement to the story.

This kind of frame was particularly well used in *My Left Foot*, when Mary read Christy's book while staying with him. This frame had its own beginning-middle-end structure, which was the growth of their relationship. It began with their meeting and moved to their developing interest in each other, then to his asking her for a date, and their going out.

The structure of the book was also used to give structure to the film. The book is divided into chapters such as "Mother," "Home," "The Artist," and so forth. These chapter headings then provided a frame for action within these sections.

The film also relied on several scene sequences for movement, such as the scene sequence of Christy's teacher's engagement, and the scene sequence of building his own room. Since much of the film was episodic, it needed all these structures to give it shape.

Time can be telescoped in a true-life story, so the flow of the story isn't constantly being interrupted by signposts such as "five years later" or "six months later." Although you may occasionally need to tell the year, it isn't always necessary. Think about the careful handling of the passage of time in *Driving Miss Daisy*. We are never told the year on the screen, but we are given considerable clues. We see the changing of the seasons. Hoke tells Boolie that it took him six days before Miss Daisy would allow him to drive her. We see a calendar on Boolie's desk that announces the year. There are birthdays and Christmases and new car models that tell us about the time change.

Visual cues also helped set time changes in *Avalon*. Although this was not a true-life story, it was loosely based on Barry Levinson's mother's family and, according to Levinson, is "seventy-five percent based on fact." In this film, notice that time changes rely on visual cues. The Thanksgiving dinners and the Fourth of July celebrations help set time frames. Sam's voiceover of "I came to America in 1914" sets the time. The growth and demise of the business shows time passing.

WHEN THERE'S NO STORY

Suppose you want to adapt a nonfiction book that contains only ideas. Sometimes there will be case studies that can be expanded, in much the same way you'd expand a short story, in order to find a plot. Many times, however, you will need to treat the material as if you were writing an original screenplay, and create a totally new story line. *On the Waterfront, Chinatown,* and *The French Connection,* all based on articles, are examples of this technique. A number of television films, such as *Games Mother Never Taught You: Corporate Gamesmanship for Women* and *Having It All,* have also been based on nonfiction books.

With any material, fiction or nonfiction, there are easy adaptations and difficult ones. If you find the dramatic arcs, scene sequences, and three-act structure, it's a good indication that the adaptation will work. If there isn't a story line, I would seriously reconsider trying to adapt the material, unless you're willing to make a number of changes to make it work. If the story doesn't work, the theme and characters won't be able to create an effective film by themselves.

At the same time, don't give up on a story because the arcs are subtle or unclear, or the story line slim. You may need to build up the story, switch the order of scenes to create greater momentum, cut some subplots that aren't going anywhere, or even create a story line to reinforce your theme and characters, but you can often make these changes without destroying the essence of the material.

Anything is possible if you understand the concept behind storytelling. There are many ways of telling a story, there are many ways of applying these concepts. Warning signs don't necessarily mean you shouldn't do a certain project. But do make sure you're able to resolve the problems before spending thousands of dollars on an option, or millions of dollars on a film.

CASE STUDY:
The Phantom of the Opera

In 1990 Warner Brothers announced that they were going to adapt Andrew Lloyd Webber's long-running musical *The Phantom of the Opera* to film. It was due to be released in December 1991—about the time of the publication of this book. Several months later, the filming was delayed, with no specific future date set for the film's release.

While writing this book, I began looking for a play or book that we could discuss before it was adapted. It would serve as an example of ways to think through a project, analyzing the strengths and weaknesses inherent in the material. Since many of you are probably familiar with the *Phantom* story, this seemed like a good choice. In the next four chapters, we will discuss this musical in relation to the script elements of story, character, theme, and style.

In 1911 Gaston Leroux wrote a novel called *The Phantom of the Opera*. A number of films have been adapted from the book, including the Lon Chaney version in 1925, the Nelson Eddy version in 1943, and at least one version in every decade since the 1960's.

The Warner Brothers plan, however, was not to go back to the novel, but to adapt the Andrew Lloyd Webber musical. Here is a brief synopsis of that story line.

The Story

Christine is a singer and dancer in the chorus of the Paris Opera. In secret, she has been tutored by a mysterious figure at the opera house (the Phantom) who would like to see her perform as the lead. When the leading lady, Carlotta, is almost hurt by a falling backdrop (let loose by the Phantom), she refuses to perform. Christine is the only one prepared for the role and performs beautifully.

It so happens that her childhood friend, Raoul, is in the audience that night and becomes reacquainted with her, eventually falling in love with her.

After the performance, Christine's "Angel of Music"—the Phantom, whom she equates with the spirit of her dead father—takes her to his lair deep within the opera house.

He's obsessively in love with her and becomes jealous when he sees her growing interest in Raoul. He sees this interest as a betrayal, and determines to cause "a disaster beyond your imagination." At the end of Act One (the play is performed in two acts with one intermission), a disaster does occur—a chandelier falls at Christine's feet.

At the beginning of Act Two, Raoul and Christine have entered into a secret engagement, although she still fears the revenge of the Phantom. The Phantom, who has been silent for six months, returns, insisting that the opera he's been writing be staged at the opera house. Raoul, the police, and the managers of the opera house determine to use the opera to ensnare the

Phantom and destroy him. Their plan goes awry, and the Phantom captures Christine, and then Raoul, and threatens to kill Raoul unless Christine stays with him. She realizes the distortion of the Phantom's soul, but in an act of courage she chooses to kiss him. The Phantom allows both Christine and Raoul to leave, and disappears before the mob can find him.

Analysis

At first glance there is much in this story line that shows a strong, well-structured story. Although the play is written in two acts, it still contains the three-act structure with a beginning, middle, and end. The analysis begins by identifying what would be the Third Act of the film. From this story line we can see that the performance of the Phantom's opera, the chase, and the threat to Christine and Raoul have all the makings of a strong Third Act with high stakes, jeopardy, action, and a clear dramatic buildup to a strong climactic scene. This last sequence is cohesive, focusing on one main event so the action won't dissipate. In terms of the Third Act of the film, there doesn't seem to be any implicit story problem that would interfere with a workable adaptation.

Much of the middle of the story is only implied in the play. There's a six-month period of time between the play's Act One and Act Two, during which time Christine and Raoul renew their relationship, fall in love, and become engaged. This development is combined with the implied development of Christine's movement away from the Phantom, which is interpreted by him as a betrayal. These implied scenes could be created for the film, adding character and story development to create the film's second act. There is some danger in this, however, since this middle section of the film would need to develop two relationship plot lines—that of Christine and the Phantom and another of Christine and Raoul. Part of Act Two in a movie could be created by expanding the growth of the Christine-Raoul relationship, which is currently taking place offstage.

Act One, however, could present some problems. The play begins with the sale of the opera house in 1905 and the auctioning of various stage props and artifacts discovered in the building. The action then flashes back to 1881 to the middle of a rehearsal for an opera. Christine is introduced as a singer in the company who comes to the forefront because she is the only one who can take over the part when Carlotta refuses to sing. At the beginning of the play there is little emphasis on her; rather, it is on the context of the opera rehearsal. When we do find out more about Christine, this information is conveyed through what she says about herself, rather than through images or actions.

This works fine in the play, but Christine's "telling about herself" is not cinematic. Although the context of the opera is clear, the context of Christine is less clear, and nothing in the material implies a method for introducing Christine in a clearer, more cinematic way.

Christine seems to be the central character in the play, since most of the action revolves around her. A case could be made for the Phantom being the main character in the play, although I don't think that would be workable for a film. In the novel, Raoul is the central character. In most of the *Phantom* films, Christine is. If this is the choice made for the film, there would need to be more clarity about her introduction. When do we first see her? How will her importance as the central character be established? What do we need to know about her before we learn about her place in the story?

Act One is further complicated because there are three major backstories that need to be established for this story line to work. Christine's backstory relates to the death of her father. She responds to the Phantom because she thinks that it's the spirit of her father. Without this backstory information, her response may seem naive and not believable. Raoul's backstory tells us that he had once known Christine, and is meeting her again. We are not seeing their first meeting, but a meeting where he remembers her. This backstory could be changed for the film, since there's no reason why he needs to know her in the past in order to fall in love with her in the present. The Phantom's backstory relates how he came to be deformed, how he yearns for love, why he's living in the depths of the opera house, and why he's driven to revenge and murder.

The obvious approach to this backstory material would be through flashbacks. But this means considerable flashback material about three different story lines. Although obvious, this is also the most predictable and the least interesting technique. It also creates problems, since a flashback usually means we're "going inside someone's head" as she or he remembers a certain incident. Usually in a film all flashbacks are from one point of view, that of the main character. Even if flashbacks were used for the main character, how would the other backstory information be conveyed?

Since the setting of the story is very tight (in the opera house), any flashbacks are going to open the story up so that possibly the only time we are away from the opera will be when we're in the past. This could very easily work against the style of a story that stays within the context of the opera house. And it could create flashbacks that are informational rather than dramatic.

Conveying the backstory through dialogue is not a cinematic or dramatic way to get across such information. This is another alternative, but not a very interesting one, unless lines can be kept to a minimum.

One could decide to start the film with scenes of Christine as a young girl, or even scenes of the Phantom's backstory. But in making that choice, one character's backstory would be introduced, and the other backstories would still need to be handled somewhere in the material. From these examples, we can see that the play is a bit "backstory-heavy." This is a problem that can be solved—but it needs to be solved deftly and creatively.

Analyzing the story line raises the questions, What is the A story and what are the subplots? At first glance it looks as if the important story line is about the relationship between the Phantom and Christine, which could lead to a decision to make this the A story. But earlier in this chapter we discussed the dangers of that approach. If the relationship story is the B story, then which is the A story?

Since we're defining the A story by movement and direction, if we analyze where the movement is coming from we can look to the end of the story to see how this A story might be defined.

We know in the last section (probably Act Three of the film) that the police and the people at the opera house want to capture the Phantom and put a stop to his threats and to the killings. We know that the Phantom has traditionally manipulated the owners of the opera house—insisting that his box be kept free at the theatre and that he be paid a salary. And we know that the middle of the story shows a conflict between his wishes and the wishes of the new owners of the opera house.

This story line can give good movement to the film, provided that it's clear throughout. It is really a story line that could be defined as "trying to stop the Phantom" and the Phantom "trying to remain in control." Elements of stopping the Phantom include such actions as the owner's decision to refuse to pay him, to permit others to sit in his box seat, and not to go along with his casting demands. The Phantom's actions include his writing the opera, taking Christine, and his innumerable threats and contrivances to make others do his bidding.

In the play the strongest action on this story line occurs in Act Three, and there are only occasional references in Acts One and Two to some of these actions. This plot could easily be built up enough to give directional movement to Acts One and Two, without overpowering the relationship stories that will still take more screen time.

The play does have several subplots that can provide additional movement to the film. There is the relationship subplot of the Phantom and Christine, which is integrally connected to the A story, the relationship subplot of Christine and Raoul, and the development of their relationship.

There is also a small subplot about the Phantom writing the opera that is performed in Act Three. We see a moment in Act One when he's writing the opera, and we can presume that he is writing during the six-month period when he's silent (this occurs offstage during the play's intermission). It's a workable subplot since it can give us further information about the Phantom, can provide movement to the story, can work as a possibility for additional music in the middle of the story, and can even make us more sympathetic to the Phantom if the writer so chooses.

In analyzing the material, we can see that the problems that need to be addressed include (1) finding a way to express considerable backstory material without interfering with the style or tightness of the context and the story line; (2) adding additional development material to the relationship of Christine and Raoul; (3) clearly establishing Christine as the main character; and (4) rethinking the first two scenes of the play in order more clearly to establish the characters and context.

This adaptation will not be a matter of just "filming the play" but will take some serious rethinking and redeveloping to make the story work.

CHOOSING
THE CHARACTERS

It's difficult to know what characters are necessary to tell your story, whom to include and whom to leave out. Many writers identify with Christy Brown's frustration in the book *My Left Foot*.

> Often I'd start a story with about twenty characters in it, but about half-way through I'd become confused and wouldn't know what to do with them all, so I'd let them all be shot in turn till only about two of the main ones were left. My jotter would often become a graveyard.

A novel may be filled with fascinating characters but have far too many for a two-hour film. We've probably all had the experience of reading novels with so many characters that we had to keep flipping back and forth in order to remember who's who. Many Russian novels can be even more confusing, until we realize that Alexander and Alex and Sascha and Ivanovich are all names for the same person.

Since the characters are already created, much of the beginning work of the adaptation demands choosing, cutting, and combining characters. Once these choices have been made, the writer will need to draw on the same skills necessary to create original characters. Some characters will need to be recreated and redefined. In other stories, additional characters may need to be added to make the drama clear.

Some of the questions that need to be asked in order to make these decisions are: "Whom do you use? Whom do you cut? Whom do you refocus? What characters need to be drastically changed for film?"

FIND THE MAIN CHARACTER

In most books the protagonist is obvious—the story is about a particular character. In novels written in the third person, we watch the main character through the eyes of the writer-narrator. Sometimes the story is told by the protagonist and is written in the first person. In other cases, it is told in the first person, but the person telling the story is not the protagonist. Instead, she or he is a narrator-observor telling us a story about someone else.

In *The Great Gatsby*, by F. Scott Fitzgerald, for instance, the narrator-observor who tells us about Gatsby is Nick Carraway. In *Cross Creek*, author Marjorie Kinnan Rawlings is the narrator-observor, telling us about incidents that she observed while living at Cross Creek. And in *White Hunter, Black Heart*, Peter Viertel (both the author of the book and a character in the story) is the narrator-observor, telling us about John Wilson's egocentric desire to bag an elephant before starting to shoot a film set in Africa. John Wilson is a fictionalized character based on John Huston, who directed *The African Queen*.

Narrator-observors work well in books, partly because of the fascination and attention to detail of our narrator-guide. We gain not only understanding of the main character, but also insight into the thinking of the narrator-observor.

But none of these three films was commercially successful, and *The Great Gatsby* could easily be called a flop.

When *Cross Creek* was released in 1983, I took a special interest in the film because I had been the story analyst at EMI Films who recommended the script, written by Dalene Young. When reading it, I knew by the end of page one that I had a very special script in my hands.

The film was nominated for four Academy Awards, but it didn't do well at the box office. The producers felt it was badly distributed, while the critics gave it mediocre reviews primarily because of the passive main character, who was not integrally involved in the action. It was a perceptive point. Although distribution problems and a soft marketing campaign may indeed have been the causes of the movie's lack of success, there did seem to be an adaptation problem, since the character Marjorie was observing a story happening to someone else. True, she had her own transformations, and there was a strong subplot, but much of the action focused on the young boy with the yearling.

Other books also have narrator characters—Chief Bromden in *One Flew Over the Cuckoo's Nest*, Ed in *Deliverance*, and the young boy in *Shane*, to name three. However, these are narrator-actor characters: they comment on the main character, but they also are important players in the action.

In *Deliverance*, Lewis begins as the main character. He's the catalyst for the trip. He's the motivating character for many of Ed's decisions and actions. He's admired by Ed, commented upon, respected, looked up to. But Ed comes to the forefront during the last half of the story and becomes the active character. It's Ed who is tested, who causes the climax to happen, who himself changes, and who takes over when Lewis is wounded.

In *One Flew Over the Cuckoo's Nest*, Bromden tells the story in the novel and frames most of the scenes in the play, but he observes the action in the movie. As the film progresses, Bromden becomes more important. He begins to relate to McMurphy and he becomes a transformed character as a result of this relationship.

If the protagonist is a narrator-actor, you'll have a much

easier time adapting the material. If not, and you still want to do the adaptation, there are some methods you can use to make the narrator-observor more active.

A few years ago I worked on the adaptation of the best-selling novel *Christy*, by Catherine Marshall. The script is currently in preproduction as I finish writing this book, and the producer, Ken Wales, has told me that it looks as if all is going forward. The solutions to some of the problems we encountered in *Christy*, such as trying to make a character more active, may be helpful.

Although in the book the story is not told in the first person, Christy is something of an observor of a long-standing feud between two families in the Appalachians. The feud is good dramatic action, but it is only a small subplot taking place around Christy. Her story is religious (a search for God) and relational (her relationship with a doctor and a minister). Since the producer wanted to do a commercial film, we made the religious search a smaller subplot but carried through that theme by using images about forgiveness and reconciliation. Since the feud was the most active story line, we switched the plot and subplot, strenghtening the feud plot line and making it the A story. We looked at all the characters who were involved in the feud—whether they were active in keeping the feud going, or in trying to stop it. Whenever possible, we gave a supporting character's function to Christy, so she became more involved in the feud plot line. In the script, Christy more actively tries to resolve the problems between these feuding families. In one instance, she delivers an important note that a minor character delivers in the book. In the script, we made her see more, react more, and interact more in order to change her from a narrator-observor to the most active character.

When adapting with narrator-observors, first make sure the main character is clear, and that he or she can carry the action without the help of the narrator. If the main character is sympathetic, it will make adapting the material easier. The character of McMurphy in *Cuckoo's Nest* works well because he's sympathetic, and he can carry the story without Chief Bromden. And, since Chief Bromden becomes active, and is the recipient of McMurphy's transformation, the story becomes even more workable.

If the main character is not sympathetic (as in the case of *White Hunter, Black Heart*), look carefully at the narrator. In this film, the character Peter does have a job to do—he is the screenwriter for director John Wilson's African film, but his main function is as an observor and sometimes unwilling sidekick of Wilson. Peter is manipulated by Wilson's strong ego, making Peter seem like a pawn, and therefore weak and passive. The story might have worked better as a play, since theatre can handle ambiguities and characters who aren't always sympathetic. As a film it did not do well with either critics or audiences.

DEFINE THE CHARACTERS' FUNCTIONS

Not every character in a novel will find a home in the film. Some characters need to be cut, others refocused. How do you make these decisions? It's not just a case of choosing your favorites. You need a kind of plumb line that can test what characters will serve the film, what characters will need to be cut.

Begin by evaluating their function in the story. Every character should serve the story. Since a film tends to be more story-oriented than a novel, play, or even a true-life story, it's not unusual to find characters in these other forms that do little for the story, although they might add color, texture, or theme.

There are many ways characters serve a story. From my study of character functions I have defined four areas where characters work particularly well in film. One character can fulfill more than one of these functions, but if any character doesn't fulfill at least one of them, you need to consider cutting the character. If several characters are serving the same function, you may want to combine some.

The Storytelling Function

The characters who tell the story include the protagonist and antagonist, who set up the conflict, and catalyst characters, who carry out an action or give information to move the story forward.

These are the main characters, the "doing" characters. They make the story happen. They keep the story moving. Examples of storytelling characters are McMurphy and Nurse Ratched, Scarlett and Rhett, Lawrence of Arabia, Lewis in *Deliverance*, Jeff in *Rear Window*.

Catalyst characters are those who make decisions, add information, or create conflicts with the protagonists. Examples are the backwoodsmen who shoot at the men in *Deliverance*, George, who keeps kissing (or wanting to kiss) Lucy in *A Room with a View*, or Billie Babbitt in *One Flew Over the Cuckoo's Nest*, whose sexual activities with Candy Starr cause the climax to occur.

These active characters—protagonist, antagonist, catalyst—are the most important people in the film. If the source material doesn't contain active characters, it will be extremely difficult, perhaps even impossible, to create a workable film.

Helping to Reveal Main Characters

The helping function is carried by the love interest and confidante characters. They're needed to make the main characters more relational, and to reveal aspects of the main characters that we wouldn't learn if we only watched them "do" the story.

Most films have a love interest. Many have confidante characters. Every film doesn't need these character types, but they can be very helpful in defining and dimensionalizing the major character.

Love interest characters can be main or supporting. Love interest functions are served by Rhett and Scarlett, Lucy Honeychurch and George, and even Candy in *One Flew Over the Cuckoo's Nest*, who reveals McMurphy's sense of fun, and who gives Billy his first sexual experience. Confidantes are found in many books and plays. Mrs. Moore in *A Passage to India* is an important confidante for Adela. At times, Scarlett confides in Mammy. George confides in the angel in "The Greatest Gift" (*It's a Wonderful Life*).

Talking About, Revealing, or Embodying the Theme

Since many novels or plays are theme-oriented, they often contain characters who help the reader or audience better understand the main ideas. Such characters are not always story characters. In a film, however, it becomes important that these characters be connected to the action of the story. In *A Passage to India*, Mr. Fielding, Mrs. Moore, and Godpole serve an important thematic function. They tell us about the problems of colonization, about fairness and justice, about equality and patronization, about the values of Indian culture. But they aren't disconnected to the story. Fielding becomes integrally involved in helping Aziz, who has been accused of raping Adela, even to the extent of receiving disfavor from his countrymen. Mrs. Moore is an important witness to the event. Godpole reflects on the action, as well as on the values within their culture.

To make a thematic character in a novel or play work for the adaptation, you may be able to give him or her a story function. Perhaps the character can also be a catalyst, or a confidante.

Adding Color and Texture

Minor characters are often used to add color and texture. These characters are the memorable, entertaining, interesting people who round out the film—a funny waitress, an uptight hotel

THE ART OF ADAPTATION

clerk, the nervous nurse in *Cuckoo's Nest*, or the beauty shop assistant in *Steel Magnolias*.

Most of these characters also serve other functions. Some have a particular job to do, perhaps as a maid or chauffeur who helps us recognize how rich and powerful a particular character is. Or there might be a bodyguard, secretary, or receptionist who helps the protagonist do his or her job, while also adding entertainment value to the story.

In *A Room with a View*, there is a carriage driver who takes the main and supporting characters to the countryside to see a view. He's an Italian who spends much of the drive in an amorous embrace with a sexy young lady who he says is his sister. Besides being a memorable minor character who adds charm to the scene, he also serves several other functions. He serves a thematic function by revealing how uptight certain other characters are. He helps give context to the scene, by creating a sensual atmosphere that later plays out with George's kiss. He is also a catalyst character since he brings Lucy to George when she is actually looking for Mr. Beebe.

Try to preserve the special characters, if possible. If you find particularly colorful characters in a novel who don't seem to have a function, or may only have a thematic function, see if you can give them some additional function that will help the story. If audience members have read the book, they will eagerly look forward to seeing these characters in the film. But be careful with them. By itself, color won't make a workable film character.

CUT CHARACTERS

A novel can often handle many characters, even some who make very short appearances. But film audiences can only focus on a few characters in two hours. If there are too many people, they get confused. Arthur Knight's review of *The Cotton Club* in *The Hollywood Reporter* spoke to this problem. It said, "Its cast is huge, and the individual stories keep bumping into each other—

or worse, since so many of the players are unfamiliar, as time goes by, you even begin to wonder if, or when, you had met them before."

How many characters are too many? From my observations, I have noticed that most scripts seem to have three, five, or seven major characters. A film can handle many minor characters, but if we need to get to know a character, it will usually be difficult for us to keep track of more than seven people.

Let's look at a few well-known films to see who the focal characters are.

Deliverance has four focal characters, although Ed, Bobby, and Lewis are the most important. Drew dies partway through and is a bit of a shadowy figure for much of the story.

The main characters in *A Room with a View* are Lucy, George, and Cecil. The supporting characters who take focus are Mr. Beebe, Mr. Emerson, and Helen Bartlett.

Shane focuses on five characters—father, mother, Shane, son, and villain. *Gone With the Wind* focuses on four—Rhett, Scarlett, Melanie, and Ashley.

Notice that while in all these films other supporting and minor characters fill out the story, there are few focal characters.

If you do need a number of characters to tell your story, try to find contrasting physical characteristics as a help to your audience. In *Godfather III*, I had trouble distinguishing the assassin from the character who became Pope John Paul I. They had similar physical characteristics, but there had not been adequate time to clearly set them up as characters. In the review by Duane Byrge in *The Hollywood Reporter*, the film was criticized for this confusion: "Unfortunately, the film's cross-cut, highly choreographed finale may prove somewhat incomprehensible to mainstream viewers as scores of unrecognizable gunmen assassinate scores of equally gray guys."

The movie did, however, distinguish other characters well. There was the assassin who brayed like a donkey, Kreizinger with his moustache, and the tall and thin archbishop, who stood out among the stockier Pope and assassins.

Although some aspects of distinguishing among characters

hinge on casting, the writer can also write character descriptions that take potential problems into account.

COMBINE CHARACTERS

Cutting characters usually means combining characters. In many novels, there are a number of characters with similar functions. There might be several businessmen, villains, relatives, clients, or soldiers who all have some thematic importance. For film, combining characters can streamline and focus the story line. In the story "The Body" (*Stand by Me*) there were originally seven older boys who confront Vern, Gordy, Eddie, and Chris. The film focused on only four. I have always thought that it wouldn't have hurt the film *A Room with a View* to cut the Reverend Cuthbert Eager, who has no important story function and no real payoff in the story.

Combining characters does not necessarily mean adding up the qualities of two characters and giving them to one. It might mean cutting one character, but taking a line of dialogue or action of that character and giving it to another.

In the novel *Gone With the Wind* there's a scene when Ashley returns after the war. As Melanie sees him from a distance and recognizes him she joyfully runs to him. Scarlett, who has always felt that Ashley was hers, begins to run too. But she is stopped by Will, who says, "Don't spoil it. . . . After all, he's her husband, ain't he?"

Clearly it's an important line and gesture. But Will, who has an intuitive understanding about Scarlett's feelings for Ashley, doesn't exist in the film. So his line of dialogue, along with his understanding, is given to Mammy in the film.

In the adaptation of *Shoeless Joe* for the *Field of Dreams* screenplay, the character of Bluestein was combined with the character of Mark to create one buyer instead of two. Ray's brother Richard was not a buyer and didn't possess any of those qualities, but some of his reactions to the baseball field were given to Mark.

Focusing characters often means putting yourself in the audience's place, and asking how many characters we are physically able to see and keep track of through the eye of the lens. The film is framing the characters. Although both the film and the novel can show us a cast of thousands, the film works more like the theatre by focusing on a small number of people in a short amount of time.

CHOOSE SYMPATHETIC CHARACTERS

In American films, sympathetic characters are considered essential for a commercially successful film. We need to like someone well enough to be in their company for several hours. Sometimes a fascinating character can substitute for a sympathetic character. Some fascinating characters who may not be likable include Michael Corleone in *Godfather I, II,* and *III,* Henry and Tommy in *GoodFellas,* Dr. Hannibal Lecter in *Silence of the Lambs,* and Claus von Bulow in *Reversal of Fortune.*

If you have a story with negative characters, look for sympathetic supporting characters who can give audiences someone to like.

The play *The Little Foxes* contains a group of some of the nastiest, most deceptive, mean, and cruel characters in any play. Regina and her two brothers cheat each other—and everyone else. There are, however, three sympathetic supporting characters in the story: Horace, the husband who dies when Regina doesn't give him his medicine; Birdie, who is a victim of her husband's abuse and has turned to drinking; and Regina's daughter Alexandra (called Zan). Of these three, clearly Zan is the one that has the makings of a sympathetic major character.

In the film the focus changed from Regina to Zan. We see Regina's manipulation from Zan's point of view. We become aware of her decisions. Zan's emotions of bewilderment, her love of her father, and her final decision to leave her mother and not to become one of "the little foxes who eat the earth" become the positive focus of the film.

The film adds another commercial element by giving Zan a boyfriend. He's a good man, approved by her father, disliked by Regina (that immediately makes us like him: anyone whom Regina dislikes can't be all bad), and helps support the positive moral center of the film.

When choosing characters, look first for the sympathetic ones. If you don't find any, then look for the supporting characters who will capture our attention, fascinate us, engage us, and involve us. If possible, expand the role of these characters. If no one is sympathetic, be wary of the project, since audiences won't know whom to root for, whom to identify with, whom to like.

LOOK FOR CHARACTER DETAILS

It isn't enough to have sympathetic characters—they also need to be interesting. Often we are intrigued with a novel, play, or biography because of the rich characters that pull us into the story.

In the book *Out of Africa*, we are given interesting character details about Denys, some of which were translated into the film.

> Denys, who lived much by the ear, preferred hearing a tale told to reading it: . . . Denys taught me Latin, and to read the Bible and the Greek poets. . . . He also gave me my gramophone. It was a delight to my heart, it brought a new life to the farm. . . . Sometimes Denys would arrive unexpectedly at the house. He would set the gramophone going . . . the melody streaming towards me . . . would announce his presence to me, as if he had been laughing at me, as he often did.

In *White Hunter, Black Heart*, writer Peter Viertel (who is also the screenwriter character in the novel) gives us a list of details that dimensionalize the fictionalized director, John Wilson.

He made a career . . . by continually violating all the unwritten rules that govern the motion picture business. He told his bosses what he thought of them (and he was always right), he publicly abused all the women he was involved with (which is dangerous, for Hollywood is a very moral, middle-class town), he supported doubtful political causes (on the basis of integrity and not because of a romantic, adolescent political conviction), he drank in excess (and he certainly became less charming when he did so), he made a great many wonderful pictures, very few of which made any money at the box office (which is the most dangerous thing a man can do in Hollywood), and he spent all his money (which is a dangerous thing to do anywhere). . . . Actors, writers, and even producers have occasionally tried what he did day in and day out and they have all ended badly: . . . Perhaps they lacked his talent, but I don't think that is it. I think they lacked the magic, almost divine ability he had to land on his feet.

Other character touches from films come to mind: John Merrick's love of Shakespare in *The Elephant Man*, Claire Zachanassian's collecting a pet panther and husbands in *The Visit*, or Ouiser's devotion to her dog in *Steel Magnolias*.

IDENTIFY THE CONFLICT

Since conflict is essential for drama, most films focus on conflicts between two people. The most dramatic conflict you can have in a film is a conflict of action. Many of the most commercially successful adaptations focus on actions where one character has to outwit or outshoot another. We see these kinds of actions in films such as *Die Hard 2*, *Total Recall*, *Jaws*, or *Silence of the Lambs*.

But conflict does not always need to be between two people with different behaviors or actions. It may occur between two people with different attitudes and philosophies. These attitudes can be about child rearing, how to handle a situation, whether to take a new job, or whether and whom to marry.

In *Out of Africa* you may remember a discussion between Karen Blixen (better known as the writer Isak Dinesen) and Denys Finch-Hatton about marriage. She thought they should get married. He saw no reason for marriage. This conflict was expressed in the book *Silence Will Speak* by Errol Trzebinski, which was one of the original source books for the film.

> The dream that held [Karen] captive and of which she would never be able to speak, was the eternal hope that one day she would become Denys Finch-Hatton's wife. But Denys belonged to the wild nomadic world and he never intended to marry anyone. . . . Anyone who attempted to rein him in or set limitations to his freedom would lose him.

This conflict in the film was acted out in a static but rich relational scene around a campfire.

KAREN

Do you ever get lonely?

DENYS

Sometimes.

KAREN

Do you ever wonder if I'm lonely? . . . Bror has asked me for a divorce. He's found someone that he wants to marry. I just thought we might do that someday.

DENYS

What? Divorce? . . . How would a wedding change things?

KAREN

I would have someone of my own.

DENYS

No. You wouldn't. . . .

KAREN

When you go away, you don't always go away on safari.

DENYS

No.

KAREN

You just want to be away.

DENYS

It's not meant to hurt you.

KAREN

It does.

DENYS

Karen, I'm with you because I choose to be with you. I won't be closer to you, I won't love you more because of a piece of paper.

Here is a conflict over attitudes about marriage that helped define and reveal the characters of Denys and Karen.

Sometimes a novel or short story is an exploration of the thoughts and feelings of a character reflecting on a situation. Sometimes conflict is slight, or nonexistent; in such a case you'll need to create it. This may mean creating new scenes that don't exist in the book. It may mean looking for implied conflict in the book and creating a scene around it or it may mean strengthening the conflict that is there.

As you're choosing your characters, look carefully for ones that are essentially dramatic. These are the characters who have a conflict with someone. If the conflict is only within a character rather than between characters, it will create problems in the adaptation, since inner conflict is difficult to show in film.

You can also find conflict by looking for the emotional moments within a story that move you, the moments where characters feel deeply about something or someone. These are the sometimes gut-wrenching moments when characters are hurt, angry, frustrated, or fearful. Such emotions usually imply a conflict with someone. If the characters are hurt, someone probably hurt them. If they're angry or fearful, they are angry at someone or fearful of someone. Although they may be only talking about these fears and this anger, a scene can be created that expresses these feelings in relationship to someone else.

Emotional moments connect the audience to the character, just as they connect the reader to the story. If characters move you to tears in the story, they may have that ability within the film. If characters are afraid, the audience potentially can also be afraid for them.

I have never yet been able to read Melanie's death scene in *Gone With the Wind* without crying. But I can't get through her death scene in the film without crying, either.

I cry whenever Nettie returns to Celie in the film *The Color Purple*. Although the description in the book may not have this same effect, it does contain emotional words that can be translated into film:

> By now my heart is in my mouth and I can't move. I'm so scared I don't know what to do. Feel like my mind stuck. I try to speak, nothing come. Try to git up, almost fall. . . . When Nettie's foot come down on the porch I almost die. . . . Then us both start to moan and cry. Us totter toward one nother like us use to do when us was babies. Then us feel so weak when us touch, us knock each other down. But what us care? Us sit and lay there on the porch inside each other's arms.

IF YOU LOVE THEM, KEEP THEM

When you read a novel or see a play, chances are it is the characters you like, not just a story. That usually means the potential is there for the movie audience to like them too. You will probably still need to transform these characters for film. You may need to make them more active. Or add more conflict. Or bring out the emotions more. Or bring them into relationships they only talk about in the story. You may need to add further character details to fill them out. You may need to cut some characters in order to give focus to the more important ones. Although the story needs to move us, it's the characters who are going to engage us. The characters that added color and texture to the book or play are also capable of adding this richness to the film.

APPLICATION

The Phantom of the Opera contains strong dramatic characters that have worked well on stage. There are three major characters, Christine, the Phantom, and Raoul, with supporting characters of Carlotta (the prima donna of the opera), the managers of the opera house, Meg (a confidante for Christine), Christine's father (who is mentioned in the play but never seen), and minor characters such as the police officers, other singers and dancers, audience members, and so forth.

The number of characters is not overwhelming, and since the character focus in plays and films is often similar, the audience should have no problem keeping everyone's function and role clear.

There is plenty of conflict in the Phantom story. There's conflict between Raoul and the Phantom, between the Phantom and Christine, between Christine and Carlotta. There is a conflict of attitudes between Christine and Raoul and between Christine and Meg, her friend, in relationship to how they think about the Phantom. There's Christine's inner conflict as she confronts her feelings for the Phantom and makes choices, and there's conflict between her love of Raoul and her compassion for the Phantom.

There's also conflict between the two managers about what to do with the Phantom, whether to perform his opera, how to run the opera house, how to handle the prima donna. There is no end to the amount of conflict that could be played between characters.

There is considerable emotional weight to the entire story, too, since it is concerned with highly charged emotional issues such as revenge, guilt, betrayal, deceit, anger, frustration, love won and lost, and with emotions within and between characters.

On these levels, the play has everything going for it. So where are the problems? The play shows Christine caught between two powerful men. On the stage (certainly in the production that I saw), the Phantom was a much stronger, more dramatic, more original, more fascinating character than Raoul. Raoul can easily seem like a stereotypical "handsome leading man" with little detailing or uniqueness. Yet the Christine-Raoul relationship is the one the audience must root for. In the adaptation, Raoul needs to be strong enough to balance the fascination we will probably have with the Phantom.

As the play proceeds we need to change our allegiance (if we had any) from the Phantom to Raoul. If we want Christine to be happy in love, the play takes the viewpoint that it's Christine's relationship with Raoul that can fulfull her. We may not want the Phantom to die, but we certainly don't want him to kill Raoul and overcome Christine. Yet Christine's growing love of Raoul could be interpreted as a betrayal. How are we to keep our sympathies with Christine if we think she's betrayed the Phantom? How are we to sympathize with Raoul if we think he's unfair, deceitful, or without compassion in his handling of the Phantom?

In the play, the power of the music, the spectacle, and the story line made it unnecessary for me to come to terms with my own attitude toward the Phantom. But the closeness, intimacy, and bigger-than-life aspect of film demands an emotional response from the audience. How are we to think about the Phantom? Are we to be sympathetic toward him because of his deformity, and then change our sympathies as he becomes vengeful? Are we to understand his obsession with Christine, or fear for her because of his obsession? Are we to pity him? Are we to be fascinated or repelled by him?

Christine could also present some character problems. Her belief that the Phantom is the spirit of her father could seem incredible. Her receptivity to the Phantom could make her seem overly naive. Keeping her engagement secret could make her seem like a passive character who allows others to make decisions for her. Her betrayal of him could take sympathy away from her. As a woman, she is a product of her times, the late nineteenth and early twentieth century. How is the modern-day woman moviegoer to sympathize and identify with Christine?

Although I could accept Christine as a theatrical figure, I have many questions about her that would need to be addressed for film. How ambitious is she? Is she simply responsive to the Phantom's help, does she want to play the lead because she loves singing, or is she truly ambitious? Are her feelings for the Phantom entirely a result of her belief that he's the spirit of her father or do they arise from compassion or fear? Or simply from gratitude for his help?

This is further complicated because Christine is at the mercy of most of the action, rather than effecting the action. Others are active, but she is the passive recipient of their guiding, leading, pushing, and pulling. Although Christine is the focal character around whom and because of whom the action occurs, it is the decisions of Raoul and the Phantom that determine the direction of the action, thereby weakening the central character of Christine.

Christine does make decisions, but when I saw the play I had difficulty seeing them clearly. When I read the libretto, listened to the music many times, and discussed it with others who had seen the play, her decisions became clearer, although they still seemed overpowered by the more active decisions of other characters. Since film usually demands more active characters than a play, some of this adaptation would need to include careful tracking of Christine's actions, balancing them with the strong actions of the Phantom and Raoul. This would not necessarily mean making her more physically active. It would probably involve, instead, focusing and balancing her emotional conflicts and decisions.

All three of these characters have their roots in nineteenth-century melodrama. Although much more richly detailed, the villain, the hero, and the "sweet young thing" can still be seen. If they are too much within this melodrama mold, the characters can be one-dimensional and we can lose our identification with them. (I felt this was true of Raoul, and somewhat true of Christine in the play.) If they are completely removed from these roots, and they become too realistic, too much like our own age in terms of attitudes and actions, they become characters without a context. Certainly they don't belong to the modern world, nor is this meant to be a realistic film. The writer would need to find the balance between the nineteenth-century character and the late-twentieth-century audience.

Although the elements are here for strong film characters, some rethinking would need to be done about the characteristics of individual characters and the interactions among Christine, Raoul, and the Phantom. Otherwise it could be a film whose characters seem removed from us, who don't speak to us.

7

EXPLORING THE THEME

Every good film, novel, play, and story is about something. There's a theme that winds its way through the material, an idea that deepens the story line and characters.

Novels and plays tend to be more theme-oriented than films. Novels have more time to discuss and explore the theme directly through narration and description that tell us what the story is really about. Plays, with their emphasis on character and dialogue, are often written specifically to explore the human condition. Most successful films, however, tend to be more story-oriented. True, many Soviet and European films place their focus on the theme, not the story. Many Australian and New Zealand films put their emphasis on character. Often these films receive critical acclaim and play in art houses. However, in this book we are not writing about art films, but about films that play to mainstream audiences. Audiences are often impatient with the static quality of thematic or totally character-driven films. Such films may have rich images and great insight into the human condition, but they usually lack movement and direction. The audience response is often that they are slow-paced and tedious, even when they are only ninety minutes long.

But films that are merely story lines also don't do well with audiences. The best action-adventures or thrillers or dramas or comedies will still contain a theme or underlying idea. The story might be about good and evil, or about justice, or about manipulation, or the integrity of the hero who faces a corrupt system. A comedy might explore the nature of love, or ambition, or the hazards of modern life. A light comedy such as *A Room with a View* is about identity, about a young woman finding herself. *Deliverance* contains themes of civilization versus the primitive in the wildness of nature and in human nature. *Amadeus* is about mediocrity and jealousy, *High Noon* about integrity, and *The Burning Bed* about victimization and abuse.

Translating the theme from one medium to another is not always an easy matter, for the way one person handles a theme can be very different from the way another works out an idea. The process first demands deciding on the theme, and then finding dramatic, rather than literary, means to explore it.

Although there may be a number of themes in any story, either one central theme will come to the forefront or the other themes will be aspects of one overriding idea. The strongest films will emphasize one theme that resonates through story, character, and images.

When there are several themes in a story, it's up to the writer and the director to make some decision about what theme to emphasize. When I was directing the play *The Visit* by Friedrich Dürrenmatt as my dissertation project, I decided to play out the theme of the process of spiritual corruption. At the end of one performance, another director came up to me and said that when he directed the play, he emphasized the theme of the dangers of capitalism. Both themes were implied in the material, but the play became more cohesive by focusing on one main idea.

Sometimes a film explores connected themes, using the A story to explore, perhaps, the nature of identity, but using subplots to explore related themes such as integrity (integrity means knowing who we are and taking a stand), love (when we find our identity we are better able to reach out to others), perhaps even justice (people who stand up for what they believe are often taking a stand for justice for others, as well as for themselves).

If you use a variety of themes, make sure they're related to each other, with each subtheme dimensionalizing the main theme. Sometimes writers create unconnected themes, such as an A story about love, a B story about greed, a C story about reincarnation, and a D story about community. If there's not one clear theme that moves throughout the story, the meaning of the film won't be clear.

FINDING THE THEME

Obviously, before you can decide how to translate the theme, you need to find it. Themes can be conveyed a number of different ways in a book. To identify themes, look at these areas:

1. The narration of the writer
2. The dialogue
3. The story choices that the writer has made
4. Choices that the characters make
5. Images used in description that can be translated into cinematic images

The Narration

In early novels, such as *Tom Jones* by Henry Fielding, the theme was readily apparent. The writer simply stopped every now and then to have a chat with the reader about what the story was really about.

In Chapter 11 of *Tom Jones*, called "Containing Many Rules, and Some Examples Concerning Falling in Love: Descriptions of Beauty, and other More Prudential Inducements to Matrimony," Fielding discusses his theme of love. "It hath been observed by wise men or women, I forget which, that all persons are doomed to be in love once in their lives. No particular season is, as I remember, assigned to this; but the age at which Miss Bridget was arrived ['past thirty'] seems to me as proper a period as any to be fixed on for this purpose." Fielding then continues to discuss aspects of love, the differences between the loves of older women and younger women, and between reasonable and superficial passions.

Contemporary novels are more subtle in their approach. The writer uses the narration to imply and explore the theme. In *A Room with a View* the narrator gives us insights into Lucy's struggle to find her identity by mentioning that she did not even know her own opinions about works of art. "She walked about disdainfully [in Florence], unwilling to be enthusiastic over monuments of uncertain authorship or date. There was no one even to tell her which, of all the sepulchral slabs that paved the nave and transepts, was the one that was really beautiful, the one that had been most praised by Mr. Ruskin."

Many novels are written in the first person. The narrator who tells the story is also a character in the story. In *Deliverance*, *Postcards from the Edge*, *Stand by Me*, *One Flew Over the Cuckoo's Nest*, *To Kill a Mockingbird*, *The Great Gatsby*, and *Rear Window* a character tells the story to the reader. This gives us an opportunity to get inside the head of the character, as he or she thinks through the meaning of events.

In *Deliverance*, Ed reflects upon the inconsequence of his life:

> Before I made a move, though, I sat for maybe twenty seconds, failing to feel my heart beat, though at that moment I wanted to. The feeling of the inconsequence of whatever I would do, of anything I would pick up or think about or turn to see was that that moment being set in the very bone marrow. . . . It was the old, mortal, helpless, time-terrified human feeling, just the same.

This feeling motivates him to join Lewis, Drew, and Bobby on a journey into the wilderness. Although this exploration of the theme isn't as direct as Henry Fielding's, nevertheless it's quite clear that the narrator is taking time away from the telling of the story to reflect upon its meaning.

Dialogue

In many novels there is one character who embodies the theme. In *Deliverance* Lewis wants to live on the edge, testing himself against the elements, desiring to be prepared so that he can win in life-and-death situations. Ed tells the story of Lewis, who, "a year or two before, had stumbled and crawled for three miles to get out of the woods and back to his car and then driven it home using a stick to work the gas because his right ankle was so painfully broken."

Lewis motivates his friends by discussing why it's important they go on this trip down the river. He unrolls the map of the wilderness, saying, "When they take another survey and re-work this map . . . all this in here will be blue. . . . This whole valley will be under water. But right now it's wild. And I mean wild; . . . We really ought to go up there before the real estate people get hold of it and make it over into one of their heavens."

The film begins with the men already driving into the wilderness, but using much of this same dialogue to discuss their motivation for the trip.

In *A Room with a View* the theme is stated a number of times in the film by reworking dialogue from the book. In both the book and the film Mr. Emerson says, "My poor boy has brains, but he's very muddled. . . . I don't require you to fall in love with my boy, but I do hope you can help him. If anything can keep him from brooding—and about what? . . . 'Things don't fit.' . . . And make my boy realize that at the side of the everlasting why, there is a yes and a yes and a yes."

In the film, the identity theme is also conveyed when George realizes that he—and Lucy—have changed as a result of encountering passion and violence in Florence.

GEORGE

Something tremendous has happened.

LUCY

Well, thank you again. How quickly these accidents do happen, and then one returns to the old life.

GEORGE

I don't. Something tremendous has happened to me—and to you.

When adapting dialogue, be aware of the actual words as well as the subtext of what's being said. This scene is rich with the subtext of George's sense of connection to Lucy and Lucy's lack of awareness, of Lucy drawing away from the impact of her experience and George realizing he's had a life-changing experience. Sometimes the dialogue can't be directly translated to film, but the subtext could be used as a guide for other dialogue.

Story Choices

The writer plays God when writing a novel, or script, or play. The writer has the opportunity to decide what happens to the characters, and these choices help the reader or audience understand the theme. If a writer is writing about love and there's a happy ending for the couple, that might imply a theme "ultimately love will win" or "love conquers all." If there's not a happy ending, the theme becomes something different—perhaps that "we don't always get what we want," or "love is difficult to find" or "love ultimately is destructive."

In *Deliverance*, James Dickey makes a number of story decisions. With each story decision, we might ask, "Why did he choose this decision instead of another?" "How does each decision create a different theme?"

We might ask: Why did he decide that the story takes place right before a dam is built? Why did he decide that this particular dam would destroy the wilderness? Why couldn't the men take a river trip on a well-traveled river? How does the imminent dam help communicate the theme of the contrast of civilization with the primitive?

Why did he decide that Drew had to get killed? Why did he decide to have the canoes tip over? Why did Bobby have to get raped? Why was it important that Ed watch the rape? Why did he decide to have Lewis kill the rapist, rather than Ed, or Drew, or even Bobby?

What was Dickey trying to explore by having the men confront so many dangers in the wilderness? How does he explore his theme by choosing natural dangers, as well as dangers from the mountain men?

In *A Room with a View*, why did E. M. Forster have Lucy watch a murder? Why did he decide to have George kiss her, Miss Lavish observe the kiss and then proceed to tell Miss Bartlett about it? What do these actions tell us about Lucy's coming of age? About her discovery of her real identity?

In *The Little Foxes*, Regina allows her husband to die because she ignores his pleas for his medicine. Why did Lillian Hellman choose to let him die, rather than to be incapacitated, or in a coma? What does that story choice tell us about the theme of corruption and manipulation?

Making one event happen rather than another gives a whole new set of meanings to the story.

Characters' Choices

Throughout any story, characters decide to do one thing rather than another. Sometimes these choices are moral choices that help to express themes of good and evil, or themes of integrity and identity. At other times, these decisions tell us about the values driving the characters, or about their ambitions, desires, and goals.

With good writers, these characters' choices are not arbitrary. In *Deliverance*, we get insight into the theme by asking, "Why did Ed choose to kill the mountain man, rather than to make a run for it through the rapids?"

In *Amadeus*, why did Salieri choose to actively destroy Mozart through his masquerade, rather than by spreading rumors or swallowing his pride and retreating into obscurity?

In *High Noon*, what was the significance of the sheriff standing up to the gunslingers? What does that say about the nature of integrity?

Each of these character's choices not only add new dimensions to the character, but help the writer communicate theme.

Story Descriptions and Images

In a novel or short story, the writer needs to use a certain amount of description to give the reader the context, and to build the story. Although some of this description simply tells us where we are, or what the character is wearing, some of the description is carefully chosen to build an image.

Pictures have meaning. And the pictures that the writer chooses to show are pictures that can help convey an idea. Sometimes a story contains a great many light images—daylight, the sun, bright light. At other times a story uses images of night and darkness to communicate ideas about corruption, evil, or decay.

Deliverance uses images of ugliness, disease, danger, and brokenness to tell us about the nature of the primitive, applying it to both people and the place:

> In the few times I had ever been in the rural South I had been struck by the number of missing fingers. . . . There had also been several people with some form of crippling or twisting illness, and some blind or one-eyed. . . . And so many snakebites deep in the woods as one stepped over a rotten log, so many domestic animals suddenly turning and crushing one against the splintering side of a barn stall. . . . But I was there, and there was no way

for me to escape, except by water, from the country of nine-fingered people.

Writers will often build images by repeating the same image, by adding details to the original image, and by using contrasting images.

In *Gone With the Wind*, the repetition of images of the death of the Old South helps the reader understand the changes from a period of romance and graciousness to one of corruption and pragmatism.

In *A Room with a View*, the writer and filmmaker build up images of passion, sensuality, and violence by first showing images of statues in violent poses, then the fight and the killing, and then they present a number of sensual scenes, such as the scene with the carriage driver and his amorous companion, the scene of George kissing Lucy, and the scene of George walking home in the rain. All of these images bring Lucy out of her safe existence, where others defined her, into experiences that force her to define herself.

Many stories contrast images. *Deliverance* contrasts wildnerness images that contain beauty—"We were among trees now, lots of them. . . . I was surprised at how much color there was in them. . . . I had no notion what the trees were, but they were flaming"—with the wilderness images of ugliness and decay and violence.

The pictures that the writer selects become important means for communicating the theme. Although, in films, many images will be brought to the material by the director, if they aren't at least implied in the adaptation, the director won't have anything to work with.

METHODS FOR IDENTIFYING THE THEME

When I'm called into a project at the story stage, before the writing of the script, I usually start by looking at the structure of the story. Secondly, I want to see if the story choices also convey the theme (or, with some changes, can be reworked to strengthen the theme).

I'm a list maker. My work as a script consultant is very analytical, so making lists of story events, character choices, thematic statements and images is particularly helpful for me to break down a book in order to evaluate the material.

For instance, if I were working with *A Room with a View*, I might begin marking, or listing, some of the identity statements that E. M. Forster mentions. I would mark both narration and dialogue, such as "Lucy, who had not yet acquired decency, . . . rose to her feet, exclaiming 'Oh, Why, it's Mr. Beebe," and "A few minutes ago she had been all high spirits, talking as a woman of culture, and half persuading herself that she was full of originality," and Mr. Emerson's words "My dear, I think that you are repeating what you have heard older people say."

Several statements about Lucy's piano playing let us know that she has a Beethovenesque passion hidden within her, if she could only let it out.

> Some sonatas of Beethoven are written tragic . . . yet they can triumph or despair as the player decides, and Lucy had decided that they should triumph. . . . Mr. Beebe . . . pondered over this illogical element in Miss Honeychurch . . . and made a remark, 'If Miss Honeychurch ever takes to live as she plays, it will be very exciting—both for us and for her.

From this small list, it's possible to see that the theme emphasizes Lucy's lack of identity. And already there is some dialogue that is usable, some comments that are purely literary and not necessary to adapt, and at least one statement about her piano playing that can be turned almost word-for-word into a comment by Mr. Beebe on that subject.

Further on in the book, we can see that for Lucy, learning about her identity involves first making a wrong decision to be engaged to Cecil, and then making a right decision for George, as she learns who she is and what she wants. Although the book has a great deal of narration about the theme, it is clear that the theme is reinforced by choices that can be translated into drama.

If as a writer you find this list-making too logical and analytical, you may find it more helpful to read the story and then free-associate with it. When you finish reading, what images remain in your head? If there aren't any, chances are it's not a very visual story, and images will need to be created for the translation. What fascinates you about the material? What associations do you make with the theme? Does it apply in some way to your own life? If so, what other ideas do you bring to this theme? Is the theme universal, or does it only apply to a small number of people?

A Room with a View might make you begin to think of your own grappling for identity when you were Lucy's age. You might identify with George, who believes that "things don't fit" and has to learn to say yes to the universe. Try to think of certain situations, people, and events that helped you understand yourself. These ideas will also help to clarify whether you are working with a universal and accessible theme.

Many writers and producers turn to novels and plays to find material for film specifically because the themes are often deeper, more dimensional, more unique than in many original scripts. But in film more than in any other medium the theme needs to be carefully balanced with the story and characters. If it is presented through abstractions or overwhelms the action the film can become static, talky, philosophical, pedantic, cerebral. If the theme works through the action and character revelations and images, it can make the film more accessible, more involving, and ultimately more successful.

TRANSLATING THEMES INTO FILM

If the theme is completely conveyed through narration in the book, the adaptation will be difficult, perhaps close to impossible. What the author talks about can often be too "on-the-nose" and pedantic to put into dialogue. Some narration simply can't be translated. It contains no story or character choices, and there is no way to create an image around the idea. Under those circumstances, careful thought needs to be given as to whether adaptation is worth the difficulty, when there is little chance of success.

If the narration is in the first person, the translation will usually be easier. Some narration can be adapted into dialogue, some even into images. But this will depend on how much of this narration is inner dialogue that could become talky, how much is simply philosophizing, and how much, with some re-working, can be dramatic and relational.

The film *Deliverance* handled this translation well (James Dickey wrote both the book and the screenplay). Much of the film dialogue expands on narration and images in the book, like Lewis's comment on the building of the dam: "You know what's going to happen, they're going to rape the whole land-scape. . . . It's the last chance to see the river . . . the end of the line. . . . Sometimes you have to lose yourself before you find anything. . . . Machines are going to fail and the system's going to fail—and then survival. Whoever has the ability to survive."

Dialogue in the film picks up the idea of the "nine-fingered" backwoods people with the line "Talk about genetic deficiencies."

Lewis says, "I don't believe in insurance, there's no risk."

The wilderness-versus-civilization theme is highlighted with the line "What law? Where is the law?" as the men decide what to do with the dead body, and reflect on the new rules in the wilderness.

Story choices become one of the best indications of the adaptability of one form to another. Action is the key to drama, and if most of the story is reflection, pondering, and philosophizing, either by writer or character, there will not be sufficient action to move the story and engage the audience.

Character choices can provide some of the action, but in novels and stories there can be both active and reflective choices. Novels are particularly good at conveying the subtle, small, inner choices that characters can make that both reveal character and inspire transformations. Although these more subtle choices can add shading and detailing to a character, they are not strong enough to rely on as the major focus of a film.

If the character choices are active, there will be a better chance of success, since the choices will contribute to the story and action of the film. If they are inner and reflective, the translation may be more difficult.

Film is an image medium. It relies strongly on the picture to move the story, reveal character, and express the theme. Sometimes a novel may contain few images, and yet can potentially make an easy translation into film because the images are implied. Other novels may contain a great deal of description, but none of it strong enough to create vital cinematic images.

FINDING THEMES IN TRUE-LIFE STORIES

In a novel or play, the original author has already interpreted the material. The theme is usually apparent and has already been worked out. In a true-life story, finding the theme is more difficult because a life contains more potential themes than any book or play. If a screenwriter options a published biography, the original author has already made some thematic choices, which makes the screenwriter's job easier. But many films are based on more than one book, and some are based on interviews and research material that must be sorted through and refined by the writer.

In these cases, the story you decide to tell will depend partly on the theme you want to express. Where is the meaning in a life? What do you want to say about this person's choices? What issues do they raise? Will you focus on the person's triumph over adversity, thereby making it a "triumph of the human spirit" story? Will you focus on his or her rise and fall, thereby showing that "crime doesn't pay" or "power corrupts" or "ambition unchecked leads to disaster"? Will you show his or her struggle to succeed in order to show that "determination pays off"?

Clarifying the theme means continually sorting through story material to see what events can prove your theme. If you choose "ambition unchecked leads to disaster," you will be selecting incidents that show an ambitious person being brought down. Perhaps there will be incidents showing ambitious choices made to the detriment of integrity or honesty. Perhaps there will be a subplot showing how professional ambition ruined a person's family life or friendships.

As with novels and plays, you'll also be looking for images, dialogue by or about the person, as well as the person's own reflections about life to discover and express the theme.

NONFICTION
MATERIAL BASED ON AN IDEA

In most cases when you're adapting nonfiction material based on an idea, you're adapting the theme. You are looking for the idea within the book or article and creating an original screenplay that expresses this idea.

Sometimes you might decide to option a book because the title is snappy and evocative and could make the project salable. With a psychological self-help book you might find a case study that could be the jumping-off point for creating a character or situation or even a story line.

These are the most difficult adaptations because you're trying to conform to a particular idea and yet you're writing an original screenplay. You don't have the guidance of a story and characters, but you also don't have the freedom of creating an original screenplay because you're trying to stay true to a particular idea and often to a particular title.

The more creative you can be with this material, the better chance you have of making this kind of adaptation work. I'm sure that Dr. David Ruben did not expect Woody Allen to create the anxious talking sperm for his adaptation of Ruben's *Every-*

thing You Wanted to Know About Sex but Were Afraid to Ask, and yet this is one of the most workable nonfiction adaptations because Allen did not allow the content and style of the material to limit him.

Another workable adaptation was the television movie of *Having It All* based on Helen Gurley Brown's book. The idea of a woman having job, husband, and happiness was explored in the film through a main character who not only has a successful job but a husband on each coast. This is not what Helen Gurley Brown had in mind as an example of "having it all," but her idea served as a leaping-off place for creating a comic approach to the material.

If you decide to do this kind of adaptation, think of it as creating an original screenplay. You will probably need to do a certain amount of brainstorming about what the theme means to you personally and what it might mean to audiences. You might think about characters you know who exemplify this idea or story lines that might work with the idea.

Two books that have been optioned by several producers and writers over a long period of time have been *The Great American Man Shortage* and *Women Who Love Too Much*. No one, however, has yet found the right approach to the books in spite of the good ideas and the strong "hook" within both the titles and the material.

APPLICATION

The Phantom of the Opera is rich with themes. There are the psychological themes of obsession, revenge, betrayal, power, manipulation, and courageous love. There are universal themes of good against evil and dark versus light. There are mythic echoes of the Beauty and the Beast story, the Faust story, the story of Oedipus, of Orpheus, and the hero's journey.

The setting of the play and the dialogue imply other themes of illusion versus truth, about masking and unmasking one's true nature, about seeing into the heart. And many images are carried through sound, particularly through the music and the lyrics.

All of these themes suggest images; any number of them would be workable for a director. The journey image was beautifully shown in the play, as we watched the Phantom leading Christine to his lair, moving back and forth across the stage as if through a maze. (I understand two doubles were used to achieve this effect.)

The contrast of the color and brightness of the stage with the darkness and concealment of the Phantom's lair is both thematic and imagistic. This contrast is further reinforced through the lyrics of the Phantom's song—"The Music of the Night"—when he calls upon Christine's "dark side" to respond to his music.

There are several images in the play that suggest illusion versus truth and could be further expanded upon. Christine disappears through a mirror. There are mirrors in the dressing rooms. A theatre implies curtains, frames, and a difference between reality and illusion.

There are a number of mask images. Not only does the Phantom wear a mask, but the second act of the play begins with the song "Masquerade" as the chorus sings about the spectacle of the colorful masks that disguise the truth. There is no lack of images, dialogue, and music that can reinforce this theme.

Although all of the above themes are carried through images, dialogue, and story movement and should translate well into film, the chosen theme also needs to be personal. We need to be able to identify with the events and see their significance for our own lives. To understand the personal theme, we must look at the focal characters: the Phantom, Raoul, and Christine.

These three characters all take a journey in this story. The Phantom's journey takes him into some degree of light and love, and then into increasing darkness and revenge. Christine's journey takes her from seduction to escape. And Raoul's journey takes him into love and heroic action to save his beloved.

Some of these journeys echo myths and fairy tales. Most fairy tales show a heroic journey as one character overcomes any number of obstacles that get in the way. Many myths have images of entrapment, manipulation, and overcoming evil. When exploring a theme such as this, one might explore it by researching fairy tales that echo each of the characters, perhaps by reading some material on the meaning of myth such as Joseph Campbell's *The Hero with a Thousand Faces* or *The Power of Myth* or by watching sections of the Bill Moyers series on Campbell. Clarifying the myth can help a writer pull out elements that may be latent in the story, but can be developed.

When looking for myths that can help us understand the Phantom, we might think of the Beauty and the Beast story or the Grimms' fairy tale "The Man in the Bearskin." In these stories, though, the character's ugliness covered up a good soul. The Phantom thinks of himself as having a good and loving soul; in actuality, his soul is tortured, despairing, enraged, and vengeful. This suggests a personal theme related to the Phantom about the potential of both love and hate to change our actions and our souls. It also suggests some identification between audience and character. Recently I spoke to someone who had seen the play six times and asked him what kept drawing him to it. He emphasized the compassion he felt for the Phantom, the feeling that we have all felt ugly and unworthy at some point in our lives and have probably all experienced unrequited love.

Christine is under the power of both sides of the Phantom's soul. At its most basic, the story is a horror story about the Phantom's obsession with Christine, about how he terrorizes her and about her rescue by the heroic and loving Raoul. It is also about the shattering of her illusions. Christine is a key character who has something to teach us about our own experiences and reactions to obsession, darkness, or manipulation.

We can experience several areas of identification with Christine. Most of us have at some time felt under someone's spell. We don't always see clearly. Many of us have probably been in love with people who weren't good for us. Perhaps we felt we could save the beloved's soul, only eventually to discover the power of their shadow. Many of us can identify with the choices between darkness and light. Like Christine, on some level we also might have had to make choices about whether we'd be "a bride of darkness or a bride of the light."

There certainly is seduction, obsession, and darkness in our world and in our lives. Although these themes are not all equally clear in the play, they are contained in the material. If the writer, director, and actors can bring these themes into focus, there will be sufficient areas of identification between audience and film.

CREATING AND SHADING STYLE, MOOD, AND TONE

Most workable films are realistic. The realistic style is the most accessible to mass audiences, the most easily understood, and the clearest. It's like real life.

Few films use styles other than realism. Those that do have rarely been box office successes. Think of the black comedies *Crimes of the Heart* or *Prizzi's Honor*, the absurdist (expressionist) *After Hours*, or the overblown style of *Bonfire of the Vanities*. Although the first three did receive some critical acclaim, they were not box office successes. However, not all nonrealistic films have failed. *Dick Tracy*, *Roger Rabbit*, and *Batman* have proved that certain nonrealistic styles, done well, can be successful. Many European films have been critically (and sometimes commercially) acclaimed for their use of distinctive style—the existential style of *Blow-Up*, the exaggerations of Fellini, the symbolism of Ingmar Bergman.

What is style? And why is style so difficult to adapt from one medium to another?

DEFINING STYLE

Style is the particular way that a film is executed. It's separate from the content of the material. Style is not the subject matter, the story line, the theme, or the characters; it is the particular way that these elements are presented. Two thousand years ago, Aristotle said, "It's not enough to know what to say, but it is necessary also to know how to say it." Before we can begin to understand the problems of translating the style, it's important to understand exactly what style is, in both a book and a film.

Style is a broad stroke. It gives us the big picture, the overall feel of the film. Tone, mood, and shading are progressively more subtle strokes. Together, these four elements cause a certain emotional response from the audience. In order to understand how these work in literature and film, let's begin by looking at how they work in areas that are more a part of our everyday life. About the time I was writing this chapter I spoke at a writers' conference held at a Victorian inn called the Horton Grand Hotel in San Diego. Inside the inn is Ida Bailey's Bar, named after a nineteenth-century madam who was said to give a spirit of fun (and pleasure) to the area a hundred years ago. The bar also had a claim to fame since Wyatt Earp had once had a drink there.

Most of you have at one time or another been in a room decorated in the Victorian style. In Ida Bailey's Bar, there are Tiffany lamps, pictures of naked women on the walls, white marble tables, and needlepoint chairs. All the furniture and pictures were carefully chosen to give an overall sense of the Victorian style. Even within this style, the interior decorator could have filled the room with a great deal of furniture or kept it rather spare. But as long as everything in the room fits within that particular style, you would recognize it as Victorian.

The word *style* is used in many art forms. We hear about acting styles. Are you going to act in the classical style? Are you going to act in the Shakespearean style?

We hear about style in terms of clothes. When we say people have style, it might be that they wear very dramatic clothes, or dress like a Brooks Brothers executive, or we might say a woman is a "Donna Karan" person, or has an "Yves St. Laurent" style.

In art, we hear about the neoclassic style, about mannerism, or romanticism. In literature, some writers write in the naturalistic style, others are Romantics, or satirical. Style is the broad stroke. The way you work with style will begin to set a mood.

RECOGNIZING THE MOOD

Mood creates an emotional response. In Ida Bailey's Bar, the mood is romantic and nostalgic, achieved through low lighting, furnishings in shades of soft pink, and quiet background music. The mood was conducive to quiet but stimulating conversation. The choices of soft pinks and sprightly music all worked together to create not just a Victorian style, but a Victorian mood.

Other Victorian moods can be created by some change in lighting, music, or color. I've been in Victorian-style ice cream parlors, where the mood is gay and fun, achieved by using brighter colors, brighter lighting. And I've been in Victorian living rooms with stiff chairs and scratchy materials, where I felt the rigidity that was also part of that period.

RESPONDING TO THE TONE

Tone is generally thought of as "attitude." We have an attitude toward ourselves, and we have an attitude toward other people. Certainly we've heard people say, "Don't use that tone of voice with me"; "I don't like your attitude"; "Don't have that chip on your shoulder"; "Don't be sarcastic"; "Don't be cynical." Or maybe you've heard the phrase "That person has an attitude."

We've also heard people make statements where the tone wasn't clear. Was it meant as a joke? Did they mean to be sarcastic?

Tone includes the attitude that we have toward ourselves, the attitude that others have toward us, and even the attitude that an onlooker can have toward any interchange they observe.

Tone can affect mood. What would happen if Ida Bailey in her old role as madam were to walk into the bar? What tone or attitude might she bring? She might exhibit a sense of humor, perhaps setting this tone by flinging her fuchsia boa and tickling the guests. Perhaps she'd be dressed like a madam of a hundred years ago, but she wouldn't take herself very seriously. Ida might show cynicism, or irritability, which she'd convey by being sharp and curt with the customers, maybe saying, "Talk to me later, I don't have time for you now." Perhaps she'd be sarcastic. Perhaps she'd have an attitude toward us where she doesn't take us seriously, but takes herself seriously. She'd see us perhaps as self-centered, as suckers, as manipulators, as exploiters. She might convey this attitude through an aside to her business partner, perhaps saying, "Overcharge him, he'll never notice." Ida might have all sorts of attitudes toward us and all sorts of attitudes toward herself, and those attitudes would begin to slightly color the otherwise romantic mood. We could say they would add another quality to this particular Victorian bar.

SHADING STYLE, MOOD, AND TONE

The mood of Ida's place and the tone will change according to how each of these specific elements are shaded. Slight changes in the visuals, music, or even the people in the bar will cause changes in the mood and tone. Maybe the interior decorator decides to add more rose color to the upholstery. Maybe she changes the pictures on the wall, or brightens the lights. These small changes in shading will make very subtle differences in the way we feel. We still have a Victorian style. We still have a romantic mood, but the mood has now been shaded. Perhaps it's shaded a little lighter, perhaps a little more colorfully.

HOW DOES THIS APPLY TO FILM?

Some styles are much more difficult to translate into film than others. Certain choices of style and tone turn audiences off, often because they are too esoteric, too difficult to understand.

I saw *Bonfire of the Vanities* with a friend who had not read the book and who did not like the film because it was "so overblown, so full of itself."

Here my friend was giving me both a style and a tone critique. The story line of *Bonfire of the Vanities* is really about an incident that does get overblown, and in that sense some aspects of the broad acting style fit the book quite well. But my friend was also adding a comment about the attitude of the actors, the makers of the film, and the audience. She sensed that the film took itself too seriously and that the filmmakers expected the audience, too, to take it seriously in spite of the broad, almost comic, acting style. And this was something that neither she nor other audience members could do.

It is not unusual for nonrealistic films to have problems gaining audiences. Certain styles may do well in books or in plays but fail in film. Black comedy has always been a difficult style to adapt. The film of Beth Henley's black comedy *Crimes of the Heart* was difficult for audiences to accept. They had trouble "getting with the style." In the story, one of the characters tries to kill herself by sticking her head in the oven, but she can't get the match lit. Later she tries to hang herself from the chandelier, but it falls down, and she proceeds to walk around dragging the chandelier by a rope behind her. If you are "with the style," you would find this funny, which it's meant to be. But it's an unusual kind of humor. It works partly as a play because theatre is a more esoteric medium than film. It generally draws literate people who have been exposed to a variety of styles. But it also works because in the theatre, the audience and actors can communicate with each other. If the audience isn't getting it, actors can shade a line slightly differently to cue the audience to laugh. They can pause, or gesture, or change a rhythm to let the audience know, "This is funny."

When I was teaching with writer Frank Pierson in Australia several years ago, he told me he thought one of the problems with *Prizzi's Honor* was the inability of the audience to understand the black comedy style. He believed this happened partly because the volume of the first three scenes was too low, and the audiences did not get it. It was meant to be funny when the young boy is given a set of brass knuckles for his twelfth birthday, but it was done with a soft, serious tone, which didn't properly cue the audience.

When nonrealistic styles fail, the films often are severely criticized specifically for their style and tone. In *The New York Times*, film critic Vincent Canby summed up the feelings of a number of critics of *Bonfire of the Vanities* when he wrote, "*The Bonfire of the Vanities* is a historical novel about a time and place in which everything and everybody had a price. . . This ecumenical approach is what gives *Bonfire* its tone. By being consistent, the novel transcends its own cynicism to become healthily skeptical. This is just what Brian de Palma's gross, unfunny movie adaptation does not do." He added, "The value (and fun) of Tom Wolfe's long, Dickensian-detailed, tirelessly satirical novel is in its democratic approach to ridicule. All men are born trashy. Those few who aren't have trashiness thrust upon them."

In a review in *The Washington Post*, Rita Kemply wrote, "In softening Tom Wolfe's scathing satire, the director has become one with the buffoons Wolfe scored in his best-seller."

Although *Bonfire* is an example of a nonrealistic style that didn't do well at the box office, *Batman, Roger Rabbit*, and *Dick Tracy* are examples of nonrealistic styles—cartoon styles—that did. All three were nominated for an Academy Award for Art Direction, a cinematic element that sets the style, mood, and tone. All were in the broad cartoon style that draws on acting, color, and action. There's nothing subtle about this style—it's broad, containing well-defined outlines of characters, without much attention paid to emotional depth. And it's a style from the mass media of comedy, books, and cartoons, so it's usually accessible to all audiences. Cartoon style is not as concerned about a character's inner life as it is about the details of colors and textures, what kind of clothes characters wear, and how they move.

Each one of these films creates a different mood, even though the general style is the same. *Batman* is dark and somber, a story of high stakes and tragic actions. It takes itself quite seriously. Personally, I was caught up in Bruce Wayne's life, particularly with the tragedy of his parents' death, and the high personal stakes.

Dick Tracy is more lighthearted, broader in its comic values. It has a tongue-in-cheek attitude toward itself. How seriously can you take Breathless Mahoney when she sings, "Sooner or Later I Always Get My Man"?

Roger Rabbit, like *Dick Tracy*, is light. It's still tongue-in-cheek, with an attitude that delights in its characters. Its affection toward its characters is combined with an underlying serious theme, actually one about racism. Eddie's attitude toward the Toons is similar to our racist attitudes toward those who are unlike ourselves, whether of a different race, religion, color, or of a different animated world.

Both *Batman* and *Bonfire of the Vanities* also take their themes seriously, perhaps more seriously than is necessary. When this happens, audiences sometimes react by distancing themselves, saying, "I don't buy it. It isn't worth such concern."

In *Roger Rabbit*, however, the movie does take its theme as seriously as it deserves to be taken. What the film is saying is important. It's said with charm and lightness, but the movie never compromises its underlying theme.

When analyzing tone, we can refer to the writer's and director's attitude toward the material, the characters' attitude toward themselves and each other, and the audience's attitude toward the film. The tone and mood of the writer and filmmaker are conveyed to the audience through visuals and dialogue in order to create the desired emotional response.

For a film to be effective, filmmakers need to get the audience into the spirit of the piece, to create a relationship so the audience is drawn in and is able to experience the same mood and tone and feeling within themselves that the filmmaker is creating in the film.

This tone is related to the shading. We often talk about "hitting the right note," or "getting the shading just right." In music, we might refer to a saxophone player darkening some sections, adding a raspy texture, or lightening a section. When looking at *Batman, Dick Tracy*, and *Roger Rabbit*, ask yourself, "Are there places where the shading starts to go off-center?"

In *Dick Tracy*, the style is clear. There are many small details that add up—the yellow raincoat, primary colors and clearly defined silhouettes, the way Dick moves, the broad outlines of the buildings, the cartoon makeup of most of the characters (although many people commented on missing the "jut-jawed" silhouette that was such a large part of Dick Tracy's character in the comics). The mood is light and fun and entertaining.

The tone is clear. The filmmakers didn't take either the characters or the situation too seriously, and the audience wasn't expected to either.

But I did have trouble with the shading of the relationships, particularly between Dick Tracy and Tess. This may have been a problem of the script, the casting, or the acting. For whatever reason, the relationship between Tess and Dick seemed to hit some wrong notes.

I sensed that Warren Beatty wanted to shade this relationship into a bit more of a realistic, romantic one, perhaps a relationship that would carry much of the emotional tone of the film. But the color and texture of romance seemed to be missing. We might say it was shaded a bit too gray, when it needed to be lighter, rosier.

We can identify when the mood and shading are off if the film is not receiving the desired emotional response. I believe I was meant to care about this couple, but I didn't. I found Tess boring, uncolorful, uninteresting. The shading seemed more balanced in the relationship between Dick Tracy and the boy. I expect it was meant to add a humanizing touch to the story— and it did. The boy was still playing within the broad cartoon style but was adding nuances of warmth and sweetness. The boy's shading seemed just right, whereas the Dick and Tess relationship seemed to be playing with the wrong note, the wrong shading, the wrong color.

Small changes in shading and nuance can effect the way the audience responds to a film. Sometimes a writer or director might need to take out a hint of sarcasm to sweeten the scene, or put in a hint of sarcasm to shade in another meaning to the line. Perhaps the music needs to be slightly different—lighter or more melodic—in order to set the right feeling for a scene. Maybe an acting style needs to be changed slightly, adding more emotional nuance to a scene so the audience feels more for a character. It might mean more tears, or fewer, revealing more, or less, vulnerability in a character.

Many of these elements are determined by the director, who can use lighting, images, long shots and close-ups, scene composition, and placement of the camera in relationship to the background to make the style more intimate, or more distancing. But there is still much that a writer can and must do to balance these elements.

BALANCING STYLE ELEMENTS

As we've seen, style is one of the most difficult elements to translate. It's no wonder that some of the big failures have been films that chose a nonrealistic style and that films that have done well have usually been realistic.

The most obvious alternative is to do only films that are realistic. It's a safe choice, but it's too easy an answer. It does nothing to expand the art of filmmaking, and it does nothing to introduce audiences to more original and unique styles.

So don't be deterred from trying if you find a story you want to adapt that's written in a nonrealistic style. Just realize that it will take more thought, more consideration, more careful choices to make the film work and that you do run a higher risk of failure.

If you decide to do such an adaptation, first ask yourself how accessible the style of the original work is. Styles that are part of the mass media—cartoon, farce, humor—are usually accessible to almost everyone. The more subtle and esoteric styles, such as black comedy, absurdist, expressionistic, satiric, or ironic, will need to be handled much more carefully.

WHAT'S THE STYLE
OF YOUR SOURCE MATERIAL

In most true-life stories you'll be working with a realistic style. But many novels and plays are successful because of their more unusual styles. Finding cinematic language for what might be a literary or theatrical style can present great difficulties to the scriptwriter.

To begin with, you'll want to be aware of how the style is expressed through the elements used in your source material. If you're working from a novel, look at the words that the writer uses in both the dialogue and the narrative. The novel's style is set up through length of sentences, word usage, repetition, the use of symbolism and images, rhythm, and descriptions.

Is the writer using long, flowery sentences or short, spare ones? What kind of vocabulary choices has the writer made? Is the language formal or personal? What is the attitude of the narrator toward him- or herself? Toward the reader? Toward other characters in the story? Is it cynical, amused, angry, satiric, compassionate?

If you're working from a play, you will also be looking at the theatre space. How is the space used? Is it a one-set play? Is it fluid space, with the action moving from one side of the stage to another to suggest changes of location? Are scenes short or long?

Is the theatre space abstract or symbolic? Does the style come from a box representing a carriage or three bars representing a prison? Does the play try not to be realistic in order to communicate its theme?

When reading the source material, you're looking for clues

that will help you make decisions about how to translate the style into the vocabulary of film. Look at the following passages from *Out of Africa* and *Shane*. Both begin with a description of a place, and someone looking at a certain location. But notice how differences in their language and style point to different cinematic styles:

> I had a farm in Africa, at the foot of the Ngong Hills. The Equator runs across these highlands, a hundred miles to the north, and the farm lay at an altitude of over six thousand feet. In day-time you felt that you had got high up, near to the sun, but the early mornings and evenings were limpid and restful, and the nights were cold.

> He rode into our valley in the summer of '89. I was a kid then, barely topping the backboard of father's old chuck-wagon. I was on the upper rail of our small corral, soaking in the late afternoon sun, when I saw him far down the road where it swung into the valley from the open plain beyond.

Read these descriptions aloud to hear and feel the difference in language. Although both use some long sentences, there's a formality to Karen Blixen's language. She uses words that relax us ("limpid," "restful") and words that suggest formal conversation.

Karen Blixen is focusing on scope. Her Africa is a big land. She is able to "see" a hundred miles into the distance.

In *Shane*, the language is more informal ("a kid," "buckboard," "swung"). The focus is smaller, more intimate. The viewpoint shows smaller spaces ("upper rail of our small corral"). Although the description suggests a larger land ("the valley" and "the open plain"), we are seeing the land from the character's viewpoint, looking at some small point on the horizon.

What cinematic language is implied by these two descriptions?

Cinematic language includes the dialogue choices of the screenwriters. We would expect that the adaptor of *Shane* would use shorter sentences, more informal language, dialogue that is spare and direct and includes vulgar words or slang. The script-writer of *Out of Africa*, on the other hand, would avoid those choices.

The cinematic language of the director includes the choice of camera angles (long shots or close-ups), pacing (fast or slow, determined by length of scenes), as well as camera movement (fluid, panning a scene, or cutting back and forth rapidly within a scene). The director can also work with lighting and color (dark, light, primary color; soft, muted color; artificial lights and colors such as fluorescent lights, or outdoor, natural color and lighting).

The *Out of Africa* description implies a camera looking into the distance, showing us the scope of the land (remember the wonderful flying scene?). We might expect a number of shots that pan the landscape. And we might expect shots that focus on the scope from Karen's point of view to communicate her love of this big land.

The description in *Shane* implies more focus on the small details—a buckboard, a rail, a cabin—and more close-up shots and focus on the characters. *Out of Africa* is about the land, the plantation, the wide spaces. *Shane* is about a small family on a small plot of land, trying to claim their rights to their home.

SET UP THE STYLE IMMEDIATELY

Whatever style you choose, you will need to pay very careful attention to how it is set up. The first three minutes of this kind of movie become extremely important. If the audience isn't with you within three minutes, they probably are not going to be with you at all. That means that if you're going to do black comedy, you can't wait for your black comedy moments fifteen minutes into the movie, because the audience won't know what style they're in. It means taking them by the hand in the first minute or two of the film, letting them know right up-front: yes, this is black comedy, and you're supposed to find it funny.

When I directed comedy in college, one of my professors, Dr. Wayne Rood, used to ask me where my laughs were. He said if I didn't know, the audience wouldn't know. He recommended that I set up at least three laughs in the first few minutes of a play, figuring that the audience might not get the first one, or the second one, but by the third they would clearly receive the cue to laugh.

If you were to apply this principle to other styles, you would look for those moments at the beginning of the film that set the style. If you have a horror-comedy, look for the horror elements and the comic elements within the first few pages. If possible, combine them.

I once worked on a horror script that began with someone's head being cut off. It continued in this grisly fashion, and then it veered toward comedy with the result that the audience would not clearly know that this was a combination style. The writer and I spent a rather humorously morbid time talking about how you make a chopped-off head funny. We talked about ideas like having a headband wrapped around the head that says THINK PEACE, or a feather in the cap, or a funny earring, perhaps a dancing woman or a puppet on a string that, as the head rolls, moves back and forth.

Although this first cue would be funny, some people might not know how to accept it, since it would not be your usual funny joke. So we talked about a second cue and a third.

Sometimes with difficult styles the credit sequence can be of great help in setting it up. Perhaps you remember the credit sequence in *A Room with a View*, one of the most beautiful and classy credit sequences I've seen. The placards of credits were done in Italian calligraphy, with opera playing in the background. This set up a tone of classicism to the story, an indication of a slower pace. Then, as the film opened, there followed a series of clues that let you know the style also included tongue-in-cheek humor. These first few moments are both subtle and amusing. Miss Bartlett opens up the shutters in an Italian *pensione* and gives a deep sigh, saying, "Oh dear, we don't have a view." The subtext here is "This is terrible—there is nothing in the world worse than having a room without a view. Look at this, Lucy. Isn't this perfectly dreadful!"

When I watched the film I was ready to enjoy it, to be amused immediately, but just in case the style wasn't clear, the film-makers gave us more cues. At the dinner table Mr. Emerson makes a terrible faux pas, saying in a loud uncouth voice, "We have a room. You can have our rooms." The ladies at the table are perfectly aghast. This is not how civilized people talk. We realize the immensity of the problem: if they change rooms, perhaps dear young Lucy Honeychurch would end up sleeping in the same bed that young handsome George had slept in the night before.

In case someone still doesn't see the humor, George puts his vegetables into the shape of a question mark, questioning the meaning of existence, and turns the plate toward Lucy.

After a few more "Oh dears," the Reverend Beebe kindly offers to help negotiate this fragile situation, the trading of rooms.

Here, although the character is taking this seriously, the film-maker isn't. Throughout is the gentle, affectionate, human tone of writer Ruth Prawer Jhabvala and director James Ivory toward the subject. The style is tongue-in-cheek with a tone of affection toward the characters.

One of the most beautifully played moments of the film occurs after Lucy Honeychurch has broken off her engagement with Cecil. Here James Ivory and the actor Daniel Day-Lewis made the choice to shade the scene by playing out the human dimension, showing Cecil sadly, but with dignity, putting on his shoes. In this scene, the director chose to darken the mood just a bit so the audience feels for Cecil. But the scene is not shaded too darkly because the audience still needs to be rooting for George and Lucy. If it's shaded too much, the audience's compassion for Cecil might make the audience think that Lucy should go through with the marriage. This careful shading kept the audience's emotional reaction on the right note.

A Room with a View is an exceptionally fine film. It won the Academy Award for Best Adaptation, and was nominated for Best Picture and Best Director. But it's the kind of movie that might not have worked. If there had been a false note in this film, it would have fallen apart.

INTEGRATING THE STYLE

It's not enough simply to set up the style. The style also must be integrated and continue to move through the whole movie. Once you commit to a style, you need to stay with it throughout.

Once the filmmakers have established their tongue-in-cheek style in *A Room with a View*, they don't want to lose it. They use a number of different techniques to keep the style paramount. Think about the title chapters in various places in the movie that maintain the tone and attitude and keep us from taking it too seriously. Every once in a while the film stops to title the next section of the film. These titles (taken directly from the book) include "The Reverend Arthur Beebe, the Reverend Cuthbert Eager, Mr. Emerson, Mr. George Emerson, Miss Eleanor Lavish, Miss Charlotte Bartlett, and Miss Lucy Honeychurch Drive Out in Carriages to See a View: Italians Drive Them"; "How Miss Bartlett's Boiler Was So Troublesome"; "Lying to George"; "Lying to Cecil"; "Lying to Mr. Beebe, Mrs. Honeychurch, Freddy, and the Servants."

We've probably all seen films where the styles become a hodgepodge. In the early 1980's there was a film called *Ice Pirates*, which began with a science-fiction, almost *Star Wars* style, and then about halfway into the film moved into a very broad, funny, campy style. But by that time nobody laughed. We had not been told at the beginning that we were supposed to laugh. In spite of its original and even workable approach in the last half of the film, the movie died very quickly.

The John Hughes film *She's Having a Baby* also combined styles. It began with a serious dramatic tone, moved into a certain amount of light comedy, had a marvelously funny scene of suburbanites mowing the lawn in a broadly choreographed farcical style, moved into romanticism, and then back into drama. Chances are that this variety of unintegrated styles was partially responsible for its lack of box office success.

You must have an integrated style throughout the film. The style choice you make at the beginning will affect the choice of dialogue, images, costumes, acting style, even character and story choices. The style needs to be balanced. If the script is a horror comedy, the horror and comedy must work together. It cannot be a film with horror in some parts and comedy in a scene or two. If it's a fantasy-farce, keep both fantasy and farce present for the duration of the film.

Let the style fit the material. The Liberace docudramas contained a certain flamboyant style that worked well. If you were going to do a film about Douglas Hemmings or David Copperfield and their world of magic, you might create a magical, colorful style, perhaps adding more wonder and enchantment to the Hemmings story and more sensuality to the Copperfield film.

MORE THAN JUST STYLE

Style, in itself, won't hold an audience. When working with a project that is highly stylized, give the audience more than just the style. If they don't understand the style, they can still connect with the material through the story, theme, or characters. The film will work *in spite of* the style, and the audience can enjoy the other elements *because of* the style. There are no barriers to the audience's enjoyment.

Sometimes audiences feel that they didn't like the style because they couldn't follow the story. Or they couldn't identify with any of the characters. Or they thought the story was without meaning or substance. Audiences can only enjoy the film if all the other elements, such as story, character, and theme, are clear, as well as the expression of these elements.

One of the most important elements comes from the emotions that are elicited by the film. Audiences need to feel with and for the characters. Even though the characters will not be realistic, their emotions still need to seem real. If audiences can't connect emotionally, it will be difficult for them to sustain interest.

Think about how you connect emotionally to such highly stylized films as *Edward Scissorhands* or the films of David Lynch (*Eraserhead, Wild at Heart*) or Ken Russell (*Women in Love*).

In stylized films that work, you appreciate the art of the filmmaker while never losing sight of what is being expressed.

Setting the style, eliciting a mood, setting the right tone, and shading a scene or action are some of the most difficult aspects of adapting any material to film. These are the areas where adaptations often reach their highest level of art.

APPLICATION

The Phantom of the Opera is bigger than life. The roots of the play in the horror story and the romance implicitly give it a style that is more theatrical than realistic. There are broad characters that reinforce the style. The Phantom character is a powerful creation that can't be equated with any ordinary realistic villain. The humorous characters are also broad and theatrical, such as Carlotta and the managers of the opera house, who are people we easily laugh at. The theatrical style reinforces the mythic themes and seems to be an essential part of the power of the story. But it is not a realistic style—and it is a story that does not seem to work well within a realistic framework. In 1990 a television miniseries of *The Phantom of the Opera* used a more realistic style. Although I found the story line of that production clearer than in the play, much of the magic and power were lost.

Much of this theatrical style comes from the music. The music is passionate, emotional, melodic, soaring, compelling, and memorable. There is little dialogue—the music dominates.

How will this musical style translate into film? There has not yet been a commercially successful film where the music dominates. *Carmen* did well as an art film, but I'm sure this Phantom is meant for mainstream audiences. Other successful musicals such as *The Sound of Music, My Fair Lady,* and *Oliver!* have been stories with music. In the previous chapters I mentioned that the film of *Phantom* warranted further character and story development. These additions could easily be expressed through dialogue, giving the musical style of *Phantom* a similarity to the musical style of other successful films in this genre. Some thought could be given to the riskier stylistic choice of letting the music dominate the other elements, which would mean adding additional music where story and character need further development. The prospect is intriguing, but might not work. In spite of the power of the music, the dominance of the musical style has the potential to make the film less accessible to mainstream audiences.

The setting also sets the theatrical style. The play takes place mainly within the opera house. The settings are varied—a stage, a dressing room, the Phantom's lair, an office, the roof, the opera ball around the main staircase, a graveyard, underground passageways, beyond the lake. Setting most of the play within an opera house makes the play fluid and cohesive. In a film this limited setting could feel claustrophobic. In the play there is one setting outside the opera house, the graveyard. This implies another world outside the opera house that could be explored. With further development of the relationship of Christine and Raoul, any number of locations could be chosen to further reinforce the dark-light, underworld-versus-above-world, imprisonment-versus-freedom themes.

Although the style is not realistic, it's identifiable. We've seen many broad styles in films, including farce and broad comedy, horror, and even the theatrical styles in such musical comedies as *Gigi* and *An American in Paris*. The translation of the style could be brilliant—provided it's accessible and well worked out through the writing, directing, and art direction.

SUMMARY

The last four chapters have begun a process that you can use for the translation of any source material into film. Some of this analysis will be done unconsciously—you'll start with a feeling about whether the original story would make a viable project. Some analysis will need to be done consciously, even methodically, to ensure a successful adaptation.

In our analysis of *The Phantom of the Opera*, as with any source material, we still need to ask the essential question: "Will it work? Does this look like a viable adaptation, or are the dangers greater than the chance of success?"

In the case of *The Phantom of the Opera*, we can see that this play has many elements that should make a workable translation. But it is not without its dangers. It is by no means a "sure thing." The inherent problems we discussed, such as the need for clarity of backstory and further development of characters and story, all have to be addressed. There needs to be some thought to how to focus the theme, and how the characters will express those themes. There needs to be some refocusing and rethinking of the play, including deciding on the balance between the musical and theatrical styles. Most of the solutions, though, are implicit in the material. That is a good sign of a potentially workable adaptation.

It is hoped that as you finish the initial evaluation of your source material, you'll clearly be able to see the problems. Then, by analyzing the story, character, theme, and style you'll be able to find workable solutions. In the case of *The Phantom of the Opera*, it looks as though it has the potential to be a brilliant film—and I, for one, am eagerly awaiting its adaptation.

PART
THREE

TWICE TOLD—
TWICE SOLD

OPTIONING A STORY

I'm not a lawyer, but I know a good one. And that's one piece of information you'll need to know in order to protect your rights, and to protect whoever owns the rights to the story you want to option.

As you read this chapter, remember that what I say does not substitute for the advice of an attorney. It is true that even if you have little money available, you can still option material. Under these circumstances, you may decide to use the model option agreement on page 201 to option original source material. But the agreement is not airtight. Only an attorney can guarantee your protection.

WHAT CAN YOU OPTION?

Consider these possible scenarios. Perhaps years ago you read a little-known novel and loved it. Since then you've written one screenplay, and for your second you'd like to adapt that novel into a film. What do you do to option the material? And do you have a chance of getting the rights?

Last summer you were enraptured by your second cousin's story about her trip to the Amazon. She was the first American scientist allowed into the rain forest to evaluate possible land uses. For a short time she was a friend of Chico Mendes, who worked to save the rain forests. With the renewed interest in ecology, the subject should be both topical and dramatic and make a good film. But how do you protect your rights—and hers?

Everybody is talking about a new Off-Broadway play. You know there's currently a bidding war over the rights between 20th Century-Fox and HBO, but the playwright seems reluctant to do business with them. You'd like to get in on the action—and you think you could give better guarantees to the playwright. How do you proceed?

Stories that would make good films are everywhere. Often they're in our own backyards. In my own immediate experience there are three stories that, if I were a writer or producer, I would consider optioning.

1. Eugene Hasenfus, the mercenary who was shot down in Nicaragua, is from Marinette, Wisconsin, the city neighboring my hometown. For a short period of time I considered optioning rights to his story, because I thought he might be more apt to give me the option than a company he didn't know and might not trust. My mother knew his wife, and kept me informed about his homecoming. This was a very hot story several years ago, and the kind of true-life experience that might make a good film.

2. Sergeant Medina also lives in Marinette. You may remember that Sergeant Medina was accused, along with Lieutenant Calley, of shooting civilians during the Vietnam War. Although some people consider Vietnam to be passé as a film topic, this was a crucial incident in the Vietnam War that could possibly be made into a film. My mother used to teach his children, and had a connection that would have been useful to me if I wanted to option his rights.

3. A few years ago, a book was published called *The Cold War Romance of Lillian Hellman and John Melby*, by Robert Newman. It was the story of a long-term relationship between the well-known American playwright and an American diplomat. Because of Melby's relationship with Hellman he was believed to have Communist leanings and was called before the House Un-American Activities Committee. Soon afterward he lost his job. At no time was there any proof of any compromising circumstances, nor was there any proof that Lillian Hellman was a Communist. Yet he wouldn't deny his relationship with her, and their relationship ended his career in the diplomatic service. The book takes the viewpoint that it was John Melby who was the great love of Lillian Hellman's life, not Dashiel Hammett. If I had wanted to, I might have had a shot at obtaining the rights because I have a special connection to one of the main characters: John Melby is my husband's uncle. Shortly after the book was published Robert Greenwald Productions optioned the book, with plans for either a feature film or a television movie.

Chances are that even if you're an inexperienced writer, there are stories like these within your reach that could make good films, and might even be your entrée into film. This chapter is designed to help you understand the optioning process— how to proceed as you find books, plays, and stories that seem adaptable.

AN OPTION VERSUS A SALE

An option means that for a certain amount of time you have the exclusive right to purchase the rights to a novel, play, or true-life story. No one else can develop the material while you hold the option.

An option is the right to buy something. You want to option a project (rather than buy it) so that you have tied up the rights for the smallest expense. This gives you time to try to sell the project, without tying up all your money in one project that may or may not sell.

You do not need to option or buy a project that is in the public domain. When you decide you want to adapt a book, play, article, or true-life story, you first need to know if it is in the public domain. If not, you will then need to option or buy the material.

WHEN IS A WORK IN THE PUBLIC DOMAIN?

If the material is in the public domain you won't need an option. Public domain material covers two different areas.

Expired Copyright

Current copyright laws protect works for the life of the author plus fifty years. If you want to base a script on a book that is no longer under copyright, you should be safe. This means that there are many famous works available. Probably all of the works of Mark Twain and Jack London would be in this category, along with the novels of E. M. Forster, Jane Austen, Charlotte Brontë, Charles Dickens, or any of the other classics from the nineteenth and early twentieth centuries. Of course, there are no problems at all if you want to do a Shakespeare play.

But you need to have some knowledge of copyright law to make sure the works are in the public domain. For instance, before January 1, 1976, the copyright law protected the writer for an initial term of twenty-eight years, plus a renewal term of twenty-eight years if the author and/or heirs renewed it before the expiration of the first term.

Before optioning a book, you would need to examine whether the work was protected under the pre- or post-1976 law, and whether the original copyright term was extended for the second term. About the time of the enactment of the new law, Congress extended certain copyrights that were about to expire in the years between the late 1960's and 1976. So if you are basing your script all or in part on a book that was originally copyrighted, make sure you know for sure whether it is in the public domain.

Material That Is Part of the Public Record

Public domain also refers to the wide body of material taken from the public press, from court documents, from recorded public documents, or from public agencies. If you're writing a script about someone in the public eye who's been the subject of many articles, you may not need their rights. If you're writing about a trial, the court record may give you all the information you need.

Many true-life stories rely on public domain material. The movies about such public figures as Elvis, Liberace, and Jackie Kennedy were all done with public domain material, without getting the subjects' rights. Although one of the Liberace films was done with the cooperation of the estate, the other was not. Sometimes a producer or writer will not get principal rights, but may go after subsidiary rights, such as the rights of a friend or relative—someone who would know the principal subject well. In this case the story may be told from this person's point of view, while relying on public domain material for scenes with the principal subject.

Doing a script by using public domain material does not mean that you can't be sued. It does not get you over the legal hurdle of claims of defamation of character or of invading the right of privacy of the subjects of your story.

When the networks planned to do an unauthorized film, or a docudrama, as such TV films are called, about Elizabeth Taylor, she promised to sue—and to spare no expense. The project was dropped. When they were thinking of doing one about John De-Lorean, he also promised to sue. His story would have had other pitfalls, since he was eventually found innocent. You are particularly vulnerable when doing a story about someone accused of a crime and then found innocent, since focusing on the accusation may defame his character, or invade his right to privacy.

If you do decide to write a story about subjects who are in the public eye and are still living, you have two choices. You might decide to write the story completely from material that is part of the public record, or you can contact the persons in order to get their rights. However, if you contact them and they won't give you their rights, you may then be unable to use the material in the public domain, since the negotiation has failed. Once the contact is made, you've chosen a route that probably has only two alternatives—either the person will sell you the rights, or you can't write the story. It would be difficult to convince a court at a later date that you tried to get the rights for "added protection." The court will probably find that your attempt to obtain rights is an admission that you felt you needed those rights; therefore, doing the story without them could lead to a lawsuit.

Even though you could write the adaptation entirely from material in the public domain, you may want to get an option. Several years ago the producer Robert Radnitz wanted to do the story of Mary White, the child of William Allen White, editor of the Emporia, Kansas, newspaper. White wrote a famous essay about his daughter, who had died at a young age. This movie could have been done without obtaining any rights, since the essay was in the public domain. However, Radnitz wanted to shoot the film in Emporia, Kansas, with the full cooperation of the town. As a result, he obtained rights, even though that wasn't necessary.

Obtaining an option even though it's not necessary gives you certain advantages when writing the story. (1) It gives you the literary rights to the story, which protects you and the subject. (2) It may get you a release from any legal claims that may arise from the use of that material. For instance, if the subjects have given you their rights, they cannot then turn around and sue because they don't like the way you write their story (unless you defame them or invade their privacy). It gives you a safety net. (3) It may get you the technical assistance or the active involvement of the owner of the rights. In many cases, you will need the assistance of your subject. He or she can give you further information, insights, and even serve as technical advisor in the film, usually for an additional fee. In some cases, subjects will even play small roles in their films. Norton Baskin, Marjorie Kinnan Rawlings's husband, appeared briefly in the film *Cross Creek,* about the life of Marjorie Kinnan Rawlings (written by Dalene Young and produced by Robert Radnitz). When Shirley McLaine's book *Out on a Limb* was optioned, she was hired to play herself.

The First Amendment recognizes that biography, literature, and docudrama entitle a writer to comment on matters that are in the public record. But public domain material still carries potential dangers and traps.

LEGAL LIABILITIES IF YOU DON'T OPTION RIGHTS

When you write from public domain material you must be particularly careful about not misinterpreting, defaming, or fictionalizing. For instance, if you were to write something false and defamatory about Oliver North, even if you were working from public domain material you could still be sued for defamation. If public figures do sue, they have to prove that the work was published with actual malice, knowledge of falsity, and/or conscious disregard for the truth. If it's clear that a public figure has done something negative, you can write about that, but you can't misinterpret. If you mistakenly said something false about someone, you would not be held liable unless the public figure could prove that you had done so willfully and deliberately.

The film *Silkwood* was an exposé of the Kerr-McGee Corporation's unsafe practices in their nuclear plant. It was done without any agreements with the company. There were elaborate agreements with the estate of Karen Silkwood, with her boyfriend, and, at a later date, with her roommate (played by

Cher). Although Kerr-McGee threatened legal action, they never filed any lawsuits against the film. This was not because the producers signed a release, but because the film was so carefully produced and documented that everything attributed to Kerr-McGee, everything they were accused of doing, was sufficiently factual and verifiable that they could not mount a successful defamation case.

If you do decide to write from the public domain, you can't make up anything unless it's clearly shown to be fact. You could show a scene of Jackie Kennedy at the funeral of John F. Kennedy: that scene is in the public domain because we've seen it on television and read about it in the newspapers. But if you decided to follow this with a scene of Jackie alone in her room, or having a private conversation with her children, you would have begun to fictionalize the story, and you could get into trouble. Again, whether you are sued for this would also be dependent on what happened in that scene. Did you defame Jackie's character? Did you misinterpret? Did you cast her in a false light? You could be sued for invasion of privacy and for presenting nonfactual material without a release or an option.

Sometimes writers try to get around possible defamation charges by fictionalizing material and adding a disclaimer that "Any similarities to people living or dead are coincidental" or that the material is "inspired by a true story," but is not about any particular person. But this can also leave you open to lawsuits. As attorney Steve Rohde puts it, "One man's fictionalization is another man's falsity."

In California several years ago there was a case involving a novel called *Touching,* by Gwen Davis. To write her book, Davis attended a series of nude marathons in Topanga Canyon that were conducted by Dr. Paul Bindrim. Prior to attending the sessions she signed a contract in which she agreed not to write any material about them. *Touching* was a thinly veiled story about a series of nude marathon sessions in Topanga Canyon. She fictionalized the character of Dr. Bindrim and for dramatic purposes suggested that his particular methods of therapy had caused the death of one of the participants. Dr. Bindrim sued

Gwen Davis and her publisher, Doubleday, not only for breach of contract, but also for defamation of character. Several witnesses testified that they recognized Dr. Bindrim as the main character. At the trial, Bindrim's lawyers treated as a false statement everything that the author had done to fictionalize the character. When the character had a long white beard, and Bindrim didn't, that was false. When the character said abusive things that Bindrim didn't say, that was false. They were able to catalogue every falsity that the author claimed was fictional, and used the fiction to prove that false things had been said.

They then put witnesses on the stand who said that when they read the book they thought that the character was Paul Bindrim, even though the name of that character had been changed. Bindrim won that case. Although the damages were reduced on appeal, it stands as a warning to writers to be careful—you can libel someone through fiction.

The book *White Hunter, Black Heart*—based on the director John Huston and the events surrounding the filming of *The African Queen*—was published in the early 1950's. It was written by Peter Viertel, who also did the rewrites on the script for *The African Queen*. To Viertel John Huston was both a hero and a villain, and the book shows an egotistic director—flawed, manipulative, even cruel. In 1957 the novel was optioned, first by Hecht-Lancaster Productions, then Columbia, then Rastar. The option included a release from both John Huston and Peter Viertel to use the novel as the basis for a script, provided John Huston's name wasn't used. The film was not made until after Huston's death, and it probably couldn't have been made if the rights had not been obtained before he died, since much of the portrait was negative.

RESEARCHING PUBLIC DOMAIN MATERIAL

A writer can find out whether a book is in the public domain by asking the U.S. Copyright Office in Washington, D.C., to conduct a copyright search. There's a nominal fee and it may take a while to get the results. The address of the U.S. Copyright Office is Library of Congress, Washington, D.C. 20559; telephone (202) 479-0700.

There are also private companies that can conduct these searches. You can get faster results from them, since you can hire them on a "rush" basis if you need the information immediately. Thompson and Thompson, in Massachusetts, is a corporation that will conduct a search for you, for about $85 and up. In addition they will also search for articles, announcements, book reviews, press releases, etc. relating to the work, and/or can help you track down the owners. Their address is 500 Victory Road, North Quincy, Mass. 02171-1545; telephone (617) 479-1600.

FINDING OUT WHO HAS
THE RIGHTS TO THE STORY

If you are trying to option material that is not in the public domain, you'll need to find out who has the rights to a particular story.

If you're optioning a book, start by talking to the publisher. All major publishers have a rights and permissions department, which will tell you whether the publisher controls the motion picture rights or whether the author retains those rights. You will deal either with someone in that department or with the writer's agent, or you will be turned over directly to the author. In order to protect the author's privacy you may be asked to put your request in a letter, which will then be forwarded.

If you want to obtain the rights to a play, you can contact the Dramatists Guild; if the play is published, the publisher will probably be either Samuel French or Dramatists Play Service, both in New York City. Either they will retain the rights to the play, or they can give you the playwright's address. You may also be able to find the address of a playwright or screenwriter (or the name of the agent) through the Writers' Guild East or West.

It will usually be difficult if not impossible for a new writer to obtain the rights to a Broadway show. Many of these rights are tied up before the show even opens, often by a motion picture studio, which will have obtained the rights in the early stages of development or rehearsals. However, you may be able to obtain the rights to an Off-Broadway play. If the play is still running, you can contact the playwright through the theatre. If not, the play may be published, in which case you can get the playwright's address from the publisher.

If you find an article in a magazine that you want to option, call the magazine. Chances are the rights will be held by the writer of the article, but the magazine will usually give you the name, or forward a letter for you.

You are allowed to use specific public domain facts from the article for your story without optioning the article: historical facts cannot be copyrighted; they are in the public domain. However, the expression of the facts is copyrightable. If you did a script about the Iran-contra affair based on the facts in a newspaper article, you wouldn't need to option the article. But if you did the story from the viewpoint of attorney Brendan Sullivan, using his recollections, you would need to get his rights.

If the writer controls the rights, none of the above sources can give you an address, and you are determined to track it down, there are some other avenues to try, including public records (if you know where the writer lives) such as court transcripts and civil lawsuits. You can hire a private investigator who has access to voter records. Use your imagination. And don't bypass the phone book. You might be surprised at how easily you can find the person you want.

WHOSE LIFE IS IT, ANYWAY?

With true-life stories, once you decide that you are not going to go through the public domain you have to figure out whose story (or stories) you need to option before you can make contact with the subject.

To begin, look for the central figure in the story. If you were going to do a story about the Iran-contra affair, whose rights would you need to tell the story? Oliver North's? Ronald Reagan's? John Poindexter's? George Bush's? Robert McFarlane's? You would need to decide how you're going to tell the story. Whose point of view will you use? If you decided to tell the story from Oliver North's point of view, you might need to option the rights of his wife, of Poindexter (his superior), maybe even of McFarlane. You would probably decide that you can use public domain material for Reagan, Bush, and other public figures. You would be asking not only who's the main character, but who else is involved in the story, even in a marginal way. The number of permissions you need will depend on the perspective you take on the story.

You may want to option someone's life story, and realize that there are several books about that person. Which one do you option? If possible, option all of them, to protect yourself.

Sometimes one book is already optioned, so you option the other(s). Several years ago I consulted on a project about Edgar Cayce, based on the book *There Is a River* by Thomas Sugrue. Producer Joie Albrecht had optioned the book, but there were other books about Edgar Cayce that covered other aspects of his life and were optioned by other producers. In this case, Joie could work only with the material from the optioned book, or from public domain material about Edgar Cayce.

CAN ANYONE GO AFTER AN OPTION?

There are millions of stories out there, and they are fair game for both the new and the experienced writer, producer, or director. In fact, there are numerous examples of new writers who managed to get rights away from big companies.

Sometimes subjects of true-life stories just don't trust a studio and would rather work with someone they know personally, trusting that this person will protect their interests. Sometimes you may find that you have something in common with the subject, which will strengthen the possibility that he or she will sell you rights. Say that you're a writer who was once in the Olympics. It may be that Bruce Jenner or Mark Spitz would rather sell their rights to you than to an impersonal studio, which may not understand sports. Or you are an M.D. and a writer. Maybe Dr. Christian Barnard would be more comfortable selling you his rights, believing that you'd better understand his story.

The producers who optioned Karen Silkwood's story were not well known, in spite of the fact that her story and her death were national news. A number of people were interested in her rights, including Jane Fonda, who had read a story *Ms.* magazine had done on Silkwood. However, two young filmmakers at UCLA, Buzz Hirsch and Larry Cano, became interested in the story, realized it would make a terrific movie, and were determined to get the rights. By making some phone calls, they found Bill Silkwood, Karen's father, in Texas. They respectfully introduced themselves to him and made plans to see him. They spent several days with him, telling him that they had a financial partner with some resources, and that they wanted to tell the honest, true story of his daughter. In the end, notwithstanding the interest of many other people, they got the rights.

In the early 1980's, Columbia Pictures wanted to make the story of *Out of Africa* and had bought the rights to Karen Blixen's book of that name. This book, however, did not contain enough material to create a really workable story. Knowing this, writer Kurt Luedtke set out to option a small biography by Errol Trzbinski about the relationship of Denys Finch-Hatton and Karen Blixen, called *Silence Will Speak: A Study of the Relationship Between Denys Finch-Hatton and Karen Blixen*, hoping to use it as leverage with the studio so he could write the script. He had already written the screenplay for *Absence of Malice*, so he had a track record and was known by the studios. As it turned out, he never had to option the book. After he mentioned it in a meeting with Columbia, the studio decided to option the book and hire him to write the script. While he was writing the script he happened to meet Judith Thurman, who was then writing a biography of Isak Dinesen (as Blixen was known). Columbia optioned this biography before it was published, solely in order to keep someone else from optioning it later. They discovered, however, that it was truly a fine book, and it became their most valuable resource for doing the film.

RIGHTS TO A CONVICTED FELON'S STORY?

Suppose you want to get the rights to a true-life story about a convicted felon. Some people feel that convicted felons have no rights, and they shouldn't be making money from their crimes. In certain states, there are "Son of Sam" laws that say criminals in those states cannot make money off their crimes. If they write a book, they can't keep any profits from its sale, nor can they profit by selling their rights for a movie (these laws are being challenged in court). Most of the time the convicted individual's rights will not be necessary, since the public record will probably be adequate for your purposes. But if you want to do a scene that isn't part of the public record, you will need to try to find some documentation. Maybe you want to do a scene that shows a murderer having a party with his wife and friends the night before he killed someone. You'd first ask, "Did this ever come up in the court record? Did the wife testify to anything like this?" If she did, you might decide that the wife is now a public figure because of testifying, and the event is now part of the public record, so it can be used. A lawyer might decide, however, that she is not a public figure, and that you defamed her through the scene you showed.

You can also take a calculated risk when showing certain scenes. You might decide that your scene is so benign that it doesn't defame the wife, that you have taken many of the elements from the public record, and that this is the only time you create any scene around her. Just to protect yourself further, you decide to portray her very positively. With this in mind, you don't think you will be sued, so you create the scene. Remember, though, making someone better than she is doesn't free you legally. If you make the wife into a very good, loving wife, knowing that she wasn't, she could sue you for misrepresenting her.

PREPARING FOR THE MEETING
WITH YOUR SUBJECT

Once you've decided whose rights you need, you'll need to contact the writer of the book, play, or article, or the subject of your true-life story. Make an appointment with the person, but before you go to the meeting, make sure you're well prepared.

First, consider having a discussion with an entertainment attorney to help you strategize the meeting. It could save you considerable money later. Although lawyers are not cheap (most will cost between $150 and $350 an hour), you do want to be wary of making costly mistakes that could be avoided.

A lawyer can help you determine whose rights you need, what questions to ask, and what kind of contract you want. He or she can advise you about what to say, and what not say, and what kind of promises it's all right for you to make. The initial meeting with the writer or subject is really preparation for the next step, which will be the drafting of a specific contract or a deal memo.

Be well prepared for the meeting. You want to be in control of the interview from the beginning, and know exactly where you're headed from start to finish.

If you're optioning a book, naturally you should be familiar with it, and perhaps with other books by the same author. If you're optioning a true-life story, you should find out as much as you can about this person. Before the meeting, you should study an option agreement so you know the kinds of issues that can arise when optioning. This first meeting is going to set the stage for the whole relationship. If it is not handled well, promises may be implied that will cause difficulties when the option agreement is being executed.

Whether you use a lawyer or not, when you go to the meeting, clarify exactly what you are asking for. Try to make an agreement for the widest possible use of the material. You can tell the person, "I am trying to acquire the exclusive motion picture and television rights, and will also want to discuss cable and cassette rights and possibly stage rights to your story."

If the person's story is not already the subject of any written material (and many true-life stories are not), you may also want to acquire the publication rights, which could include books, magazines, or even feature newspaper rights. Remember, you want to be able to control this project. You don't want anyone else to come along later and acquire some of the rights because you weren't smart enough to tie them up. If you don't acquire them, someone else could do a feature story about your subject, which would create a separate group of rights that can be optioned. So get all the rights to the story. You want an exclusive option because you don't want anyone else developing the story separately. Nonexclusive rights are meaningless.

Make sure that you truthfully and candidly portray yourself. If you're a film student seeking rights, a producer with produced films, or a first-time screenwriter, say so. Give the subject your credentials and credits, and explain your situation in detail.

Share your vision with the subject. Where do you want to go with the story? What are you going to do to make the story work? Someone might want to option his or her rights to you because your vision and commitment seems better than what's being offered by others.

Emphasize the positive and deemphasize the negative, but tell the truth. If it's the only project you'll be working on for the next six months, say so. But don't make promises that you can't keep, or it could be construed as an inducement to enter into the agreement. If you lie about your commitment, or about how you're going to tell the story, you can be liable to a lawsuit for breach of contract.

You can be sued if you renege on promises about the

depiction of your subject. Some of you may recall the book or miniseries *Fatal Vision*. When Dr. Jeffrey MacDonald asked Joe McGinnis to write a book about him, McGinnis felt that the doctor was innocent and promised to depict him in a positive light. As he continued to research the story and observe MacDonald, he began to question his innocence and took a more negative viewpoint in his writing. When the book was published, MacDonald sued McGinnis for reneging on his promise. McGinnis lost the case.

Once you promise you'll depict someone in a certain way, you need to follow through on that promise, even if you change your mind once you start writing the material. These promises may have been oral rather than written, but if there are any witnesses or letters or documents that say you made a promise in order to get an option, and then didn't portray the subject in the manner promised, you can be liable for fraud or breach of contract. If you have made promises, and then try to sell the story to a studio or network, they may not honor them and you'll be in the difficult position of not being able to sell that particular story. So be careful what you promise.

In the agreement, the subject waives the right of privacy, right of publicity, and any other civil claims. Some subjects will add that you are not allowed to say anything false and defamatory about them or to depict them in any unfavorable way. Or they might allow you creative control provided you don't depict them in certain ways, such as a drug addict, an alcoholic, or a person with a bad temper (even though they may have these traits).

Be careful of promising a percentage of profit. You can tell a subject that you will use your "best efforts" to get them profit participation, but you are not in a position to promise a percentage of net profits, since that will be up to the studio. Of course, you can if you wish give them a share of your profit, if you want to take money out of your own pocket for their rights.

Be careful of contracts that promise one percent of "profits," since it's not clear whether that means net or gross. Net profit is what is left over after all bills have been paid—to the production company, the producer, the writers, and the actors as well as any deductible expenses. You can only give away what you control. You may want to add a clause that says, "I will pay you one percent of the net profits received by me, if any, after deducting and recouping any and all development and production expenses and overhead." Each of these terms will then need definition. Few people make money on percentage points, because of the studios' "creative bookkeeping"; this refers to studio practices that "prove" they haven't made a profit, even though the film may have grossed $150,000,000 or more. ("Creative bookkeeping" practices have come under scrutiny since Art Buchwald won a copyright infringement case against Paramount Studios and the film *Coming to America*, which has grossed well over $150,000,000, although Paramount Studios says it's still "in the red.") Let your subject know that you probably won't be making any extra profits, and he or she probably won't either.

If you need other rights from subsidiary characters in order to do the story, ask the subject to help you obtain these rights. Sometimes the option agreement can require a subject to get a release from his or her spouse, or parents to get releases from children. Make it clear in this meeting if you're going to need help, and ask the subject for his or her cooperation.

Follow up the meeting with a respectful letter, confirming that you and the subject have reached an agreement (if you have). This would then be followed by the actual option agreement, which both of you would sign. For your own protection, document that you met the subject and clarify what happened in the meeting. If there is ever a lawsuit, you want to have clear notes about every step in the process.

HOW LONG SHOULD THE OPTION BE?

Generally speaking, you want an option long enough for you to research a project, to write a treatment or script, and to submit it for development to a production company, studio, or network. This process can take years. It took five years to develop the *Silkwood* story, it took almost forty years for *White Hunter, Black Heart*, it's taken over twenty years to try to bring *Christy* to the screen, and it's already taken several years to work out details for *The Phantom of the Opera*. So you will want to tie up the rights for as long as possible.

You will want an option for at least one year, along with the right to renew it for a series of additional years if you so choose. At some point, in order to renew the option you may have to show that you have written a script or treatment or have a development or production commitment. Such proof shows objectively that you are still interested in the project, and that you haven't just put it on a shelf.

If you can't pay a great deal, you usually will need to have a shorter-term option. A short-term option of one to nine months will allow you a minimal amount of time to see if there's interest in your project. If someone is wary or unsure of giving you the option, he or she might give you a short option in order to see what you can do with the material, and how committed you are to making the film.

HOW MUCH, AND WHO PAYS?

Options can cost anywhere from nothing or $1 to $100,000 and more. You can sometimes get a free option on certain rights. Perhaps you've read a novel that has sold only a few copies, but you tell the author that you want to explore the possibility of turning this into an Academy Award–winning film. Maybe you've read a little-known but fascinating true-life story and want to option it. You may be an unknown, but you're planning on putting in the time and effort to develop his or her story; that's worth something to the subject—particularly if no one else has expressed interest.

Although in many states you can have a free option, it's usually a good idea to pay something for the rights, even if only

$1. This protects you, since in some states some cash compensation is necessary. In California it's not necessary if the option is in writing.

The price of the option will also depend on how much material you need to option in order to tell your story. You may need to option several books or articles to get the needed information. Sometimes you need to option the life stories of several people in order to do your film.

Chances are you are optioning the project in hopes of selling it to a studio or network, or raising independent money to produce it yourself. You are optioning the project because you love it, and because you want to guarantee your own participation in the film—as either a writer or producer.

It's important when you option a project that you first negotiate the purchase price. Simply saying that you'll "agree to agree" at a later date isn't adequate to protect yourself, since the subject might later disagree with your terms, void the contract, and go off and make a deal with someone else.

Make sure that the purchase price you write into your contract is a price that is reasonable. Typically, a studio or production company might pay about $50,000 to $100,000 for the rights of the person who will be the major character in your story. The rights of the people who will be supporting or minor characters in the story will range from nothing to $25,000.

Studios will generally pay $20,000 and up for a novel. (Writers such as Sidney Sheldon get $1,000,000 or more.)

In your contract mention the option price and the purchase price. Suppose you make a deal with the subject to purchase his or her rights for $50,000 when you exercise the option. When you sell the project, you could make a deal with the studio for $70,000 for the rights to your subject. Now, you may think of the $20,000 as profit, but you are actually paying yourself for what was probably six months or more of work, expenses, time, and talent.

Generally what you pay for your first year's option is applicable against the purchase price, but subsequent options may not be applicable. Let's say that the purchase price is $50,000 for the rights, and you pay $5,000 for a one-year option. If you sell the rights to a studio or company within one year, the $5,000 is applicable to the price, so the subject receives $45,000. But let's say it takes over a year for you to make a deal with a producer or studio. For the second year's option you pay another $5,000, but this is not applicable to the purchase price. When the rights are sold, the subject still receives $45,000, even though you've paid an extra $5,000. The rights have now cost you $55,000. You will also want a clause in the contract that says if the project has gone into development, the subjects can't pull out of the agreement. When you have done all the work, have finally closed a deal, and are ready to sell the rights, you want to make sure that the subjects don't pull out of the deal because they think they might be able to get a better price on their own.

In the option agreement for the true-life story, you will want the full cooperation of the subjects. You may want to engage them as technical consultants on the project. You'll certainly want them freely to give you information and interview time and provide you with diaries, scrapbooks, documents, insights, and entrée to others who figure in the story. However, it's dangerous to make absolute promises to them. Not everyone sells rights just for the money; often there's a hidden agenda that might be related to a desire to be part of show business. Maybe they want to write a script, or to have a role in the movie, or to be an associate producer. If you're not the producer, you don't know what this project will look like a year from now, so you can't make any promises. You can agree to "best efforts" to help them get whatever else they want out of this project.

If you want the subject(s) on the project as technical consultants, decide on their salary during the negotiations for their rights. That way you know you'll have them when you need them. At that time, specify a daily or weekly fee for their services, remembering that this will come out of your pocket. Perhaps the company or studio who buys the project will pay the fee rather than you. It might be important to tell the studio that you have these persons available to help, since most projects need technical expertise and research. If you haven't worked out a technical consulting fee beforehand, the agreement isn't binding and your subjects could desert you just when you need their help the most.

One or two of the people whose rights you need to tell the true-life story you've chosen might not give them to you. In this case, you could write them out of the story or try to write their characters from public domain material. If you had to portray a jury, and one person out of twelve wouldn't give you their rights, you could make that person the juror who sits quietly and never says anything. If you have five panelists and only four will give you their rights, the other one could just be introduced, but never have any lines of dialogue, or perhaps only say what is in the public record.

GET CREATIVE CONTROL

If you are serious about an option, you need an airtight contract that allows you to do the creative work you need to do to adapt the property. Whether you work with a lawyer or not, you will want your option agreement to give you creative control. Hopefully you want to option something because you loved it, and you will probably want to stay within the spirit of the material. But after reading most of this book, you know that adapting material usually means making changes, including some that the author of the work or subject of the true-life story might not like or understand. The author might think that you are going "to do the book," not realizing that the material will change in the adaptation. This is not to say that authors never like the films about their work (although many don't), but sometimes the film isn't successful because the writer tried to stay too close to the original material. Sometimes the best adaptations are those that keep the spirit of the original, but make many dramatic changes.

Some producers and writers make the mistake of giving script approval to the original author of a book or play, or to the subject of a true-life story. Most people have definite opinions about how they want their story told, but few have any knowledge of how to create a dramatic storyline. With script approval, they can stop or delay a project, or make demands that will ruin it, even though the film may eventually get made. You may have to give script approval if somebody is very famous (Sidney Sheldon has script approval on all the adaptations made of his books), but in most circumstances it will work against you. Although you will want to retain creative control, you can give the author or subject certain consultation rights. This means he or she does not have the right to approve the script, but can participate in discussions or meetings and give advice.

You need a contract to protect your rights so you can adapt the material as you see fit. Don't promise creative control. The decision will only return to haunt you when you're trying to do your creative work.

MISTAKES MADE IN OBTAINING RIGHTS

There are many stories of how Hollywood producers and writers descend on a person or a place in order to get rights to "hot" stories that have appeared in the media. When Reverend Thomas Bird and his mistress, Lorna Anderson, were arrested in Emporia, Kansas, for murdering their spouses, scores of producers and executives descended upon the town to try to obtain their rights (their story became the miniseries *Murder Ordained*).

When Eugene Hasenfus returned to Marinette, Wisconsin, phone calls from would-be producers came in by the dozens, and he had to get an unlisted phone number.

Although producers and writers often go after these stories hoping to sell them as television and film projects, studios and networks don't always jump right into the bidding war. They understand the complexity of docudramas and the possible pitfalls. They are particularly wary of stories where the ending is not yet known, particularly if a trial has not yet been held and the verdict is not yet in. In these cases, there's no way to know if it will make a good dramatic story with a strong climax.

Many docudramas are about events that occurred five or ten years previously, because it might have taken five or ten years to know the ending. Usually a story ends with a strong climax that resolves the issue, such as an arrest, but in addition there may be an epilogue that gives you further information, such as "He is now serving a twenty-five-year sentence in San Quentin Penitentiary" or "She is now totally recovered from her disease and is happily married, living in Carmel." You need to know the ending. Although your story may move dramatically and logically, the ending can reverse everything you've done. The ending can change the theme, the choice of characters, even the concept that sold the story in the first place.

Sometimes writers and producers make the mistake of not obtaining all the rights they need. If one person holds out on his or her rights it can destroy a project, particularly if that person is an essential character in telling the story. Occasionally somebody is asked to cooperate on a project without signing an option agreement. You start writing the script, only to have somebody else tie up your subject's rights, making it impossible for you to proceed with this aspect of your project.

Sometimes a writer or producer ties up all the necessary rights and then realizes that there are implicit legal or dramatic problems in the story. Such problems can be prevented by adequate research and story analysis.

USING A STANDARD OPTION CONTRACT

It is always preferable to work out an option agreement with the assistance of a lawyer. But in case you cannot afford one, a model option agreement follows. Deals have been made with a simple form such as this, and if you feel you can trust the person and are willing to take a risk, this is workable.

Let's say that you are Mary Jane Smith, a writer-producer

who wants to option John Doe's true-life story about his experiences flying in Korea. You want to pay him $10 for the initial agreement, which can be renewed every year for $250. The purchase price if the story becomes a film will be $15,000 for his rights. The option will begin on June 15, 1992, and can be renewed every year after that.

John Doe
Main Street
Anywhere, U.S.A.

Mary Jane Smith
Sunset Boulevard
Hollywood, California

This will confirm the understanding and agreement between you, MARY JANE SMITH, writer-producer, and myself, JOHN DOE, as follows:

1. John Doe is the sole and exclusive owner of all rights, title to, and interest in and to the story of John Doe's Experiences in Korea ("the Story") and all the incidents and occurrences in it.

2. For and in consideration of the sum of Ten ($10.00) Dollars payable to John Doe upon the signing of this letter, and for other good and valuable consideration, the receipt of which is hereby acknowledged, John Doe hereby grants to Smith an irrevocable right and option to purchase and acquire all theatrical and television motion picture rights, literary rights, and all affiliated rights relative thereto and to the Story on the terms and conditions set forth herein.

3. This option shall commence as of the date hereof and shall expire on midnight, June 15, 1993, unless extended pursuant to the provision of Paragraph 4 hereof.

4. This option may be extended for an additional year to June 15, 1994, upon the payment by Smith to Doe of

the sum of <u>Two hundred fifty ($250)</u> Dollars at any time on or before <u>June 15, 1993.</u> (The period of the option and any extensions thereof is hereinafter referred to as the "Option Period.")

5. The Option shall be exercised by written notice signed by <u>Smith</u> and delivered personally or by certified mail to <u>Doe</u> on or before the end of the Option Period to the following address: John Doe

Main Street

Anywhere, USA

6. In the event the option is exercised as aforesaid, <u>Doe</u> shall be paid the full and complete purchase price for the work in the manner and to the extent provided for in Paragraph 7 hereof.

7. In the event the option is exercised and a feature-length theatrical or television motion picture based upon the story is actually produced and made by Smith, then <u>Smith</u> agrees to pay to <u>Doe</u> the sum of <u>fifteen thousand ($15,000)</u> Dollars (purchase price) on the first (1st) day of commencement of principal photography or taping, as the case may be.

8. During the option period, <u>Doe</u> shall not assign or encumber the story nor make any commitment with respect thereto inconsistent with the terms hereunder.

9. If <u>Smith</u> fails to exercise the option as aforesaid, all of <u>Smith's</u> rights hereunder shall cease on the expiration of the option period.

10. If <u>Smith</u> duly exercises the option as aforesaid, then <u>Doe</u> agrees to execute whatever additional documents <u>Smith</u> may deem necessary in order to properly evidence and acknowledge that <u>Smith</u> is the sole and exclusive owner of all rights, title, and interest at and to the theatrical and television motion picture rights, literary rights, and affiliated rights, in and to the story.

11. This agreement and option is fully assignable by

Smith and shall be binding upon and insure to the benefit of her respective successors and assigns and the heirs, executors, and administrators of Doe.

If the above is in accord with your understanding of our agreement, please indicate the same by signing this letter in the space below.

Sincerely,

_____ Date:_____

John Doe

ACCEPTED AND AGREED TO:

By:_____ Date:_____

Mary Jane Smith

HOW TO FIND A LAWYER

Your local bar association will be able to give you names of attorneys familiar with entertainment law. You can also ask an attorney you know for recommendations.

The cost of a lawyer will vary, depending on the complexity of the option and whether you need to get rights from several people. A simple agreement with one subject can cost between $1,500 and $2,500. If that's more than you can afford, you might simply have an initial consultation with a lawyer before meeting with the subject, as I suggested earlier, and then use the basic option agreement from this chapter. If you sell the project to a studio or company, their lawyers will handle the more complex legal matters.

The option agreement will help protect you while you're developing the project. When the project nears production, you will need another form of protection—Errors and Omission Insurance.

ERRORS AND OMISSION INSURANCE

Errors and Omission (E & O) Insurance is coverage that protects the studio or network from lawsuits for defamation, invasion of privacy, violation of the right of publicity, or violation of property rights. Most readers of this book will not need to concern themselves with this insurance, but if you are doing a low-budget independent film of an adaptation, you will need to have it in order for your film to be distributed by any major distribution company. If you are selling rights to a production company or studio, you will begin working with the insurance carrier after you sell your project.

As the writer of the project, you won't be buying the insurance—the production company or studio will. But you must provide them with the information to prove that all legal requirements have been followed.

The application for this insurance requires you to disclose whether any real persons are depicted either fictionally or factually and whether any source material was used without permission, and truthfully to describe the history of the development of the script.

If a studio is sued, the E & O insurance pays for the litigation, according to what kind of policy they have. They might have a blanket policy for all pictures, or specific insurance on one picture. There might be a high deductible, or the insurance may or may not cover attorney fees. It might pay some defense costs, but not all.

If you're doing a personal story about a nonpublic event, there's a certain amount of leeway for fictionalizing certain elements, provided you have subjects' rights. If you're doing a well-known story, dramatic license is more restricted. If you don't have all the releases you need, you are even more limited. Your position will also depend on how complete the public record is, particularly if you are doing the project as a public domain story. People whom you consider public figures might claim not to be so, and you could be open to being sued as a result.

If you're not truthful in your insurance application, all your insurance can be canceled. No script will go into development unless the script is reviewed. No problems will be overlooked.

To protect yourself and your project, make sure that you have an airtight contract, that you've acquired all the rights you need for the project, and that you've documented all information. Although you won't be working with the E & O carriers until the script is moving toward production, you must be prepared for their questions as you develop the project.

AFTER YOU HAVE GAINED THE OPTION

If your option agreement for a book or a play gives you creative control, you can work with the material any way you want. You probably don't want to lose the essence and spirit of the original, but you are allowed to make changes. Novels and plays give you greater leeway than the true-life story.

If you have optioned a true-life story, you must stay within certain parameters. Some are legal—if you don't follow them you'll be sued. Others depend on whether you are doing the film for feature or for television.

Although feature films based on true stories still need to follow certain legal procedures, legal requirements for films are less rigid than those for television, and many scripts have shown considerable creativity. *Mississippi Burning* was criticized for not really telling the truth about FBI methods for bringing the murderers to justice. *Missing* was a highly fictionalized account of a coup in Chile and how it affected certain Americans living there. *The Long Walk Home* was based on the Montgomery bus boycott, but fictional characters were put into that true-life situation.

The adaptation that poses the most restrictions for a writer and/or producer is that of a true-life story for television. If you're writing a true-life story for television, you'll need to follow other criteria, which are discussed in the next chapter.

WRITING A DOCUDRAMA
FOR TELEVISION

Docudramas are a staple of television movies. Many of the highest-rated and most critically acclaimed television shows have been docudramas—including the Emmy Award winners *Eleanor and Franklin*, *Friendly Fire*, *Edward and Mrs. Simpson*, *A Woman Called Golda*, *Peter the Great*, and *Roe vs. Wade*.

Writing a docudrama presents a number of challenges since you must stay with the facts while still trying to create a dramatic story.

WHAT IS A DOCUDRAMA?

A docudrama is a dramatization based or inspired by a true-life story. A story based on a specific living person must be accurate. The writer must guard against defamation of character, misrepresenting or misinterpreting events, and all the other potential liabilities mentioned in the previous chapter. Docudramas that are "inspired by" true-life stories have much more leeway. These are based on a specific event, but are so fictionalized that virtually no one would recognize the particular people portrayed in the story.

When you're writing such a script, you are allowed to make some changes and fictionalize some material. In chapter three I mentioned that people don't live their lives in the correct dramatic order. Their relationships don't always work dramatically. Sometimes you wish that there were fewer people in their lives or that they hadn't done certain actions that contradict the theme you want to develop. As a writer of docudramas you have creative control over some of these situations.

THE NETWORKS AND YOUR DOCUDRAMA

When a project is submitted to a network, it will first go to the programming department. This department hears pitches (TV jargon for "fields proposals"), buys stories, and develops scripts. If you were pitching a project to the networks, you'd pitch it to a programming executive.

Once the network buys your project, there are three departments that must approve your script to make sure it fulfills all criteria for docudramas. The legal department checks to see that there's a strong option agreement and that all necessary rights have been obtained. The errors and omission review makes sure that the docudrama will not lead to lawsuits. The broadcast standards and practices department reviews the script to make sure the story is truthful and that the public is not misled about events that actually occurred. Each network's broadcast standards department has codified specific guidelines and rules for you to follow that protect you legally, but also give you the leeway you need to create a viable dramatic work. (See page 213 for example).

Occasionally the broadcast standards department will insist on certain story changes, not for legal reasons, but because they feel a responsibility to tell the truth and not mislead audiences. Even if the legal department says that it's all right to fictionalize some element in the script, broadcast standards executives might say that that particular piece of information is misleading and therefore needs to be changed. Many television executives believe that television has a particular responsibility to the public because television shows may be the public's only source of information on the subject. If a TV docudrama claims to be the true story or based on a true story, it's important that it really be true to the facts.

If a project is particularly problematical, the programming department might discuss it with broadcast standards before even buying it. Or they might begin the development process and then send the script to broadcast standards. It still must go to the legal department at some point in the process before it can receive the green light for production.

These television departments will distinguish between factual and historical accuracy and any inaccuracies that may give rise to legal problems. Every screenwriter probably wants his or her script to be accurate. That might be part of the screenwriter's artistic desire. But there is also a moral or journalistic obligation to write an accurate script, even though a specific inaccuracy might not cause legal problems. And there's the legal duty to write an accurate script that is legally invulnerable.

IS YOUR STORY FICTION OR FACT?

A writer or producer has to make the decision whether to present the story as nonfiction or fiction. Much of what you see on television is loosely inspired by an actual case.

The rights to a true story are often a stronger selling point for the networks than a story you have made up loosely based on facts. You might pitch a story as true, but the network might ask you to write it as a fictionalized account. Sometimes this happens because it's impossible to get all the rights. Sometimes it's too complicated to do as a true story. The decision to fictionalize it will depend, to some extent, on whether your story could have happened to a number of people or to only one person.

Earlier I mentioned Eugene Hasenfus, the mercenary who was shot down in Nicaragua. The incident was important because it led, indirectly or directly, to the Iran-contra affair. Let's say that I wanted to do this story, but couldn't get the rights I needed. I might decide to fictionalize his story by telling a story about a mercenary who was shot down in Nicaragua while delivering arms, was captured, held in prison, and finally was released through the influence of his wife. Even if I changed details in this story, I could be open to a lawsuit, because Eugene Hasenfus is the only person this has happened to. I might change his age, the kind of airplane he flew, or even change the country, but the story would still point to him.

You might decide to do a story about mercenaries flying arms not to Nicaragua but to "a Central American country." Perhaps, through research, you have discovered there are about forty men between the ages of thirty and fifty who flew these kinds of missions, although none of them were shot down and captured. You research the different incidents that happened to these men, and choose those for your story that have happened to a number of people. This would be fine. But if your character is shot down and captured, your story would now be identified as Hasenfus's story.

It would be particularly difficult to fictionalize his story because there is a great deal of public knowledge about the event. We know what he did and didn't do. We know the sequence of events. We know about his family (his brother hand-made the parachute that saved his life and his wife traveled to Nicaragua to try to free him). We know that debriefings followed. If you tried to fictionalize his story by adding a love affair with a woman in Nicaragua, and having him receive a medal from the government, he could still sue for defamation of character because that's not what happened.

By trying to fictionalize your story, you would also be weakening it. Audiences like true stories. They like knowing that something really happened. And in this case it's the specific events that make the story fascinating, not the generalized story of a "mercenary flying arms to a Central American country."

Sometimes programmers at the network will say, "We would be interested in that if it were a true story, but since it isn't a true story, we're not."

FOLLOW CHRONOLOGY IF POSSIBLE

When writing a docudrama it's important to follow the correct chronology of events, if the chronology will influence the cause and effect of these events. If it doesn't influence cause and effect, you can make some changes in the way you tell your story.

In a historical piece about World War II, you couldn't reverse the order of events, e.g., you couldn't decide that Poland was invaded after France in order to create a more interesting story. If, in a personal story about a woman's life, she met her husband in France in 1942 but you would like to put this scene in the section that takes place in 1944, it may not be a problem, particularly if you have her rights. Probably nobody would object if you put a birthday party scene in summer, even though it took place in winter, or decided that a woman visited her grandmother in May, even though she did it in June—provided that it doesn't upset an actual cause-and-effect sequence.

USE THE FACTS YOU KNOW

Under certain circumstances you can also make changes in scenes. Perhaps you're doing a murder story based on a true story. Your villain kills someone named Lila. You know how old Lila is, you know that she was picked up at the mall and was killed about three miles away. However, you don't know if the murderer and Lila talked, or what they talked about. For a docudrama, you have two choices in terms of how you write dialogue. You may decide that you won't have her talk at all. Or you may decide to create dialogue that has a basis in fact. No one is going to object if you have the killer say, "Hello, Lila." But if you started conjecturing about a conversation, deciding that she tried to persuade him not to kill her by telling him about her abuse in her childhood, you would be fictionalizing and possibly defaming the subject. Only if there is proof in the public record that she was an abused child could you create dialogue along those lines. If there is no information, you could be sued for fictionalizing facts.

Suppose you found out that this murderer had been an abused child, but you knew very little about when and how he was abused. You may be tempted to create a scene about his mother hitting him when he was three. But without sufficient information, this could lead to a charge of defamation of character, of both the murderer and his mother.

When people in broadcast standards look at a docudrama, they add up the number of total ingredients. For every scene they ask if you can prove what's fact and what's fiction. You may be developing too many fictitious elements in the scene about a boy of three, as opposed to a scene where it's a matter of record that the killer picked up this woman, lured her into his car, and probably said a few words to her. In the first case, you're making up a scene, making up dialogue for both the mother and son, and probably adding elements to both characters that are not part of the public record and can't be proved. It will depend on how much you know. If you know that the killer talked about being hit by his mother when he was three, then you have more grounds for creating such a scene.

When you write these scenes, you are creating building blocks of proven information. You are trying to balance the number of elements in the scene that you can document with elements you create.

When analyzing what scenes to add, ask yourself, "What do I know, what can I research, and what can I conjecture might have happened based on the evidence that I have?"

USE TIME COMPRESSION TO TIGHTEN

Even within the limits of a true story, you do have a certain amount of leeway. You can use time compression to move quickly from one point in time to another. If, say, a relationship actually lasted for five years, but you think it would work better if you could end it in two years, you can usually change these facts. Sometimes this helps dramatically, particularly if you want to end the relationship right before the start of something new in the person's life. Suppose the relationship actually dissipated over a period of time. Perhaps your protagonist left for Europe for a year. Although the relationship might have been kept alive through letter writing and occasional phone calls before finally dying out, it might be more dramatic to break off the relationship right before the protagonist leaves.

The broadcast standards department also approves composite characters—combining two or more characters into one. It may be that there were actually five detectives on a case, but you know it will be more dramatic to have one or two, so you look at the work that all five did and ascribe it to just one or two of them. Perhaps there were seven children in a family, but you don't want the audience to watch the movie counting children, so you reduce the number to four or five. This will still seem like a large family, but if the number of children is not important, the reduction can help clarify and keep the focus on the important issues.

Maybe someone had four wives, or worked with three businessmen, but for purposes of clarity, you decide to combine the two younger women or the three businessmen into one character. All of this is acceptable, although it is not advisable for a major character. Also, if you're doing a composite character you have to change the name. Get releases from all the subjects who make up the composite. When doing a composite character it is not acceptable to obtain a release from only one of the subjects—it must be all or none.

GUIDELINES TO FOLLOW

A network's broadcast standards and practices department prints guidelines that are issued to producers. Before the script can be produced, broadcast standards will ask you to supply copies of key substantiation materials such as books, articles, interviews, releases that have been secured, and a list of people who are not cooperating; and documentation that corroborates each element that is based upon actual events, that depicts the actions of an actual person, or that characterizes such a person. Whenever possible, they will want to know the source of any quotes that may become dialogue in the story.

If you're a new producer, they will give you a set of their guidelines to follow. The following are ABC's guidelines:

A. Composite Characters

1. If a script uses composite characters (i.e., characters that are based on two or more real individuals) the annotated script must indicate the specific individuals who have been used to create the composite. All dialogue and actions by composite characters throughout the script must be accurate with respect to the individuals making up the composite.

2. Although it is permissible to create composite characters, as defined above, no fictitious characters—other than incidental or functional characters who have no bearing on the basic plot—are to be included in the script.

3. Generally, major characters whose story lines constitute a recurring element in the script must not be composite characters.

B. Chronology

1. Chronology of events, locations, and circumstances must be accurate throughout, and supportive evidence must be submitted to this effect in the annotative script.

2. Dates and passages of time must be clearly indicated in the script, either in dialogue, by supers, dissolves, or other visual techniques.

3. Events may be telescoped, but events that never occurred cannot be invented. Telescoped events must be chronologically accurate.

C. Legal Matters

1. Where courtroom documents are relied upon for dramatic purposes, such documents must be submitted.

2. Generally, releases from individuals depicted must be obtained. A release, however, does not mean otherwise impermissible fiction will be allowed.

D. Characterization and Attitudes

1. Personal characteristics, attitudes, and demeanor must be substantiated (e.g., if a character is depicted as feisty or quarrelsome, documentation to this effect must be supplied).

2. Created dialogue, the basis of which is circumstantial, requires reasonable substantiation to establish that it fairly represents the attitudes and beliefs of the participants.

3. If a narrator is used, his or her statements must be objective without providing commentary or editorialization.

E. Controversial Subject Matter

1. In some instances, due to the sensitive nature of the subject, multiple sources of verification will be required for scenes, events, and, in some instances, specific lines. Examples of "sensitive" subject matter are sexuality, religious issues, a highly charged political event, controversial issues, a very recent event, or a script based on a famous person who is alive.

2. Programs which deal with themes which involve controversial issues of public importance shall include a balanced presentation of contrasting views on those issues within the individual program itself unless otherwise authorized by the Department of Broadcast Standards and Practices.

F. Representative Events

There are a number of disclaimers that a writer can use. Below are different disclaimers, with the names of films which fit into this category:

> The following is a recreation of (the event or story). The action is based upon court records, eyewitness accounts, reportage, personal interviews, investigative reports, official documents, etc. (Optional: The names we use are real with the exception of certain composite characters who have been given fictitious names.)
>
> (*The Missiles of October*)

> The following is a dramatization of the life of———based on the book by———and other sources. Some composite characters and time compression have been used for dramatic purposes. (*Fighting Back*)

> The following dramatization of the life of———is based on the (book) or recollections of———.
>
> (*Marilyn—The Untold Story*)

The following is a dramatization drawn from the observations of———, a witness to these events. The events are compressed for time. Certain composite characters have been given fictitious names.   (*Attica*)

This story was inspired by/based upon the life and deeds of———. This motion picture is not an attempt to reproduce actual events, although it is suggested by them. The producer intends no more than to present a dramatic story.   (*Lizzie Borden*)

Although the following film is fictionalized, it was inspired/suggested by real people and events. [This could refer to a film with a backdrop of the Vietnam or Gulf war, or an event such as the Chernobyl incident.]

HOW TO PITCH THE STORY

For television, once you get the rights to someone's story you need to decide whether to pitch it to the networks or to partner with a production company. You will usually have a better chance pitching the story to a well-known movie-of-the-week producer. Such producers have contacts with networks. They can arrange a network meeting that may be difficult for you to arrange by yourself. You also come into the meeting with more clout, because the network knows that the producer has a good sense of what's commercial and has a track record of knowing all the steps in writing and producing a television movie.

This means you need to research which television producers have done films such as yours. If it's a story involving child abuse, there are certain producers who've made a reputation doing such stories, and doing them tastefully. The same is true of crime stories and medical stories. Look for the producer's name and the name of the production company in the credits of TV movies with similar themes to yours. If the producer is Los Angeles–based, the name and phone number will often be in the telephone book, or you can find it by calling the network that aired the show, or by buying *The Pacific Coast Studio Directory*. You can order this and other industry resource books from Samuel French Bookstore, 7623 Sunset Blvd., Hollywood, Calif. 90046; telephone (213) 876-0570.

WHAT KIND OF PROJECTS INTEREST THE NETWORKS?

Let's say you are thinking of optioning a true-life story, but you want to get some sense of the network's interest. How can you discover what kinds of stories they're looking for?

Although the network's choice of programs will vary, you can get a good idea of their interest by looking at what kinds of movies are shown on which nights (some nights the networks cater more to female viewers, other nights more to male viewers). You can read the trades (*The Hollywood Reporter* and *Variety*) to find out what projects they're currently buying.

Since television primarily has a female audience, docudramas that are female-oriented will do better than male-oriented subject matter. Look for stories in which the protagonist is a woman or that deal with relationships, problems families encounter, or issues that have some social significance. The choice of subject matter for television movies has often led to jokes about the "disease of the week" or the "issue of the week" film. Such stories have been a staple for television, since they are personal stories that create strong identification with the situation on the part of the audience.

Television movies that are difficult to sell are ensemble pieces, those with sports subjects, those set in exotic locales, and period pieces (unless it's a miniseries taken from a best-seller such as *War and Remembrance* or *Shōgun*.) One also has to realize that the political, international, and economic climate will affect what the networks are buying.

During a war, the networks might be looking for more entertaining stories. People are getting enough reality from the news without looking at more violence and bad news in television films. During a recession, audiences probably won't want to watch films about a stock market crash. After a hijacking, audiences probably won't want to watch films about terrorism. Audiences have difficulty dealing with certain situations when they're in the middle of the problem. After the problem is resolved, they often welcome the opportunity to reflect on it by watching a film about the subject.

SUMMARY

Many new writers have gained an entrée into film through optioning material for very little money, and writing a terrific script. Many well-known producers have made their reputations by concentrating on adaptations. Before adapting material, you need to make sure you clearly own the rights to it so you can do with it whatever you want. Once you have the rights, you can proceed to the creative and artistic work of creating a great adaptation.

AFTERWORD

From my experience and observations, the following are the five most important concepts to keep in mind during the adaptation process.

1. There is no such thing as "a sure thing" in the art of adaptation. The popularity of a book, play, or true-life story does not guarantee a successful adaptation. On the other hand, no matter how unknown the book or true-life story, it could become a critical and commercial hit.

2. Before spending a great deal of money on optioning a project, assess the problems and your ability to solve them. If you can't do it, don't do it.

3. Be careful of adaptations that seem too easy. Easy adaptations sometimes become unoriginal and predictable films.

4. Just because an adaptation looks impossible doesn't mean it is. Anything is possible—if you can pull it off.

5. Adaptation is both an art and a craft. You need to understand the material, the problems, and the craft of screen-

writing to make the adaptation work. But no matter how much you may know about the craft of writing and adapting, it will still need your art—your creativity, insight, and talent.

I hope you have found this book practical and usable—and that it can guide you in your work. Like Michelangelo, who looked for the angel within his blocks of stone, I hope you are able to find the film within great fiction and great true-life stories. I wish you well at creating an adaptation that's as good as, if not better than, the original.

WINNERS OF
THE ACADEMY AWARD
FOR BEST PICTURE

1930–1990

1930's

All Quiet On the Western Front, 1930 (novel)
Cimarron, 1931 (novel)
Grand Hotel, 1932 (novel)
Cavalcade, 1933 (play)
It Happened One Night, 1934 (short story)
Mutiny on the Bounty, 1935 (novel)
The Great Ziegfeld, 1936 (true-life story)
The Life of Emile Zola, 1937 (true-life story)
You Can't Take It With You, 1938 (play)
Gone With the Wind, 1939 (novel)

1940's

Rebecca, 1940 (novel)
How Green Was My Valley, 1941 (novel)
Mrs. Miniver, 1942 (novel)
Casablanca, 1943 (play)

Going My Way, 1944 (original screenplay)
The Lost Weekend, 1945 (novel)
The Best Years of Our Lives, 1946 (novel)
Gentleman's Agreement, 1947 (novel)
Hamlet, 1948 (play)
All the King's Men, 1949 (novel)

1950's

All About Eve, 1950 (short story)
An American in Paris, 1951 (musical play)
The Greatest Show on Earth, 1952 (original screenplay)
From Here to Eternity, 1953 (novel)
On the Waterfront, 1954 (nonfiction article)
Marty, 1955 (teleplay)
Around the World in 80 Days, 1956 (novel)
The Bridge on the River Kwai, 1957 (novel)
Gigi, 1958 (novel/play)
Ben-Hur, 1959 (novel)

1960's

The Apartment, 1960 (original screenplay)
West Side Story, 1961 (play)
Lawrence of Arabia, 1962 (true-life story)
Tom Jones, 1963 (novel)
My Fair Lady, 1964 (play)
The Sound of Music, 1965 (musical play)
A Man for All Seasons, 1966 (play)
In the Heat of the Night, 1967 (novel)
Oliver!, 1968 (novel/musical play)
Midnight Cowboy, 1969 (novel)

1970's

Patton, 1970 (true-life story)
The French Connection, 1971 (nonfiction article)
The Godfather, 1972 (novel)
The Sting, 1973 (original screenplay)
The Godfather II, 1974 (novel)
One Flew Over the Cuckoo's Nest, 1975 (novel/play)
Rocky, 1976 (original screenplay)
Annie Hall, 1977 (original screenplay)
The Deer Hunter, 1978 (original screenplay)
Kramer vs. Kramer, 1979 (novel)

1980's

Ordinary People, 1980 (novel)
Chariots of Fire, 1981 (true-life story)
Gandhi, 1982 (true-life story)
Terms of Endearment, 1983 (novel)
Amadeus, 1984 (play)
Out of Africa, 1985 (true-life story)
Platoon, 1986 (original screenplay)
The Last Emperor, 1987 (true-life story)
Rain Man, 1988 (original screenplay)
Driving Miss Daisy, 1989 (play)

1990's

Dances With Wolves, 1990 (true-life story/novel)

WINNERS OF THE
EMMY AWARD FOR
OUTSTANDING MINISERIES AND
DRAMA/COMEDY SPECIAL

1977–1990

Roots, 1977 (book)
Eleanor and Franklin, 1977 (true-life story)

Holocaust, 1978 (book)
The Gathering, 1978 (original TV script)

Roots: The Next Generation, 1979 (book/true-life story)
Friendly Fire, 1979 (true-life story)

Edward and Mrs. Simpson, 1980 (true-life story)
The Miracle Worker, 1980 (play)

Shōgun, 1981 (novel)
Playing for Time, 1981 (true-life story)

Marco Polo, 1982 (true-life story)
A Woman Called Golda, 1982 (true-life story)

Nicholas Nickleby, 1983 (novel/play)
Special Bulletin, 1983 (original TV script, loosely based on the play *The War of the Worlds*)

Concealed Enemies, 1984 (true-life story)
Something About Amelia, 1984 (original TV script)

The Jewel in the Crown, 1985 (novel)
Do You Remember Love?, 1985 (original TV script)

Peter the Great, 1986 (book/true-life story)
Love Is Never Silent, 1986 (novel)

A Year in the Life, 1987 (original TV script)
Promise, 1987 (short story)

The Murder of Mary Phagan, 1988 (book)
Inherit the Wind, 1988 (play)

War and Remembrance, 1989 (novel)
Day One (book), and *Roe vs. Wade* (true-life story), 1989 (tie)

Drug Wars: The Camarena Story, 1990 (true-life story)
Caroline (short story), and *The Incident* (original TV script), 1990 (tie)

BIBLIOGRAPHY

Screenwriting Books

The following are well-respected and very useful screenwriting books. Although this list by no means covers the many good books on the market, these are some I am personally familiar with and, from my bookstore research, know are popular.

Blacker, Irwin. *The Elements of Screenwriting*. New York: Macmillan, 1986.

Brenner, Al. *The TV Scriptwriter's Handbook*. Cincinnati: Writers Digest Press, 1985.

Cox, Kerry, and Jurgen Wolff. *Successful Scriptwriting*. Cincinnati: Writers Digest Press, 1988.

DiMaggio, Madeline. *How to Write for Television*. New York: Prentice Hall, 1990.

Egri, Lajos. *Art of Dramatic Writing*. New York: Simon & Schuster, 1972.

Field, Syd. *Screenplay*. New York: Dell Publishing, 1984.

———. *The Screenwriter's Workbook*. New York: Dell Publishing, 1988.

Goldman, William. *Adventures in the Screen Trade*. New York: Warner Books, 1983.

Hague, Michael. *Writing Screenplays that Sell*. New York: McGraw-Hill, 1988.

King, Viki. *How to Write a Movie in Twenty-one Days*. New York: Harper & Row, 1988.

Mehring, Margaret. *The Screenplay: A Blend of Film Form and Content*. Stoneham: Focal Press, 1990.

Miller, William. *Screenwriting for Narrative Film and TV*. New York: Communication Arts Books, 1980.

Sautter, Carl. *How to Sell Your Screenplay*. New York: New Chapter Press, 1988.

Seger, Linda. *Making a Good Script Great*. Hollywood: Samuel French, 1989.

———. *Creating Unforgettable Characters*. New York: Henry Holt, 1990.

Swain, Dwight V. *Film Scriptwriting: A Practical Manual*. Stoneham: Focal Press, 1988.

Walter, Richard. *Screenwriting: The Art, Craft, and Business of Film and Television Writing*. New York: New American Library, 1988.

Whitcomb, Cynthia. *Selling Your Screenplay*. New York: Crown, 1988.

Source Materials

The following are some of the source materials referred to in this book.

Allen, Donald M. (trans.). *Four Plays by Eugene Ionesco*. New York: Grove Press, 1958.

Brown, Christy. *My Left Foot*. London: Mandarin Paperbacks, 1954.

Dickey, James. *Deliverance*. New York: Dell Publishing, 1970.

Dinesen, Isak. *Letters from Africa*. Chicago: University of Chicago Press, 1981.

———. *Out of Africa* and *Shadows on the Grass*. New York: Vintage Books, 1989.

Fielding, Henry. *Tom Jones*. New York: Random House, 1950.

Forster, E. M. *A Room with a View*. New York: Bantam Books, 1988.

Howard, Sidney. *Gone With the Wind, the Illustrated Screenplay*. London: Lorrimer Publishing, no date.

Kesey, Ken. *One Flew Over the Cuckoo's Nest*. New York: New American Library, 1962.

King, Stephen. "The Body" (from *Different Seasons*). New York: New American Library, 1982.

———. *The Dead Zone*. New York: New American Library, 1979.

Maltin, Leonard (ed.). *TV Movies and Video Guide*. New York: New American Library, 1988.

Mitchell, Margaret. *Gone With the Wind*. New York: Avon Books, 1976.

Perry, George. *The Complete Phantom of the Opera*. New York: Henry Holt, 1987.

Schaefer, Jack. *Shane*. New York: Bantam Books, 1949.

Trzebinski, Errol. *Silence Will Speak*. Chicago: University of Chicago Press, 1977.

Wager, Walter. *58 Minutes*. New York: Tor Books, 1989.

Walker, Alice. *The Color Purple*. New York: Pocket Books, 1982.

INDEX

Abstraction in theatre, 37
Academy Awards, xi
  winners of (1930–1990),
  221–223
Actors, exchange between audience and, in theatres,
  34–35
Acts, creating three, 82–83
Adam, 54
Adaptations. *See also* Characters; Story line; Style;
  Theme
  afterword on, 219–220
  changing source material in,
  8–10
  commercial viability of, 4–7
  condensing vs. expanding
  material in, 2–4
  failed, xii–xiii, 1–2
  film-to-film (*see* Film-to-
  film adaptations)

of novels (*see* Novel adaptations)
optioning for (*see* Optioning
  stories for adaptation)
statistics on, xi–xii
successes of, xii–xiii
television (*see* Television docudramas)
of theatre (*see* Theatre adaptations)
this book on, xiii–xv
of true-life stories (*see* True-
  life story adaptations)
African Queen, The, xi, 91, 119,
  185
After Hours, 156
All About Eve, 3, 222,
Always, 66, 67, 70
Amadeus, xiv, 5, 42, 139, 145,
  223
Arc of story line, 91–93